Four Ordinary Women

Four Ordinary Women exemplifies the resilience of the human spirit. These essays are forged of grit and honesty and speak to all of us.

> —**Stephen R. Covey,** author, *The 7 Habits of Highly Effective People* and *The 8th Habit: From Effectiveness to Greatness*

Just as there are no normal families, so there are no ordinary women, and, despite its engaging title, this book proves that. Each of the four women who participated in this intriguing project is unique and each, thus, resists being labeled as ordinary or labeled as anything other than endlessly interesting. What these women show is that we all have our stories to tell because we all have been both blessed and battered by life. Readers will find countless points of intersection with their thoughts and experiences because we all share a common humanity. But readers will not simply be looking in a mirror here at their own lives played out by another. Rather, they will find new insights into - common experiences.

> —**Bill Tammeus**, Faith Columnist, *The Kansas City Star*

These four ordinary women have given us a book that is both brave and inspiring. By turns funny and sad, serious and flippant, impassioned and reflective, this collection of short pieces on a variety of subjects provides a glimpse into the lives and experiences of these women. Their commitment to honesty is praiseworthy, and one hopes that their example will serve to inspire others throughout the country to come together to share their lives in writing.

> —**Brian Bowles, Ph.D.**, Philosopher and Counselor

These writers have engaged in a remarkable process of self-discovery and insight resulting in an enlightening peek into the human family and the far-reaching effects of the family's predictable patterns and repetitions.

> —**Dori Moore**, Family Systems Therapist

Four Ordinary Women is an extraordinary journey! What a gift to find not only one woman sharing her life in such a real and honest way but all four! I found myself relating to each woman at different times as I read this book and in different places of their lives and in mine. A wonderful and heartfelt work of love that is obvious on every unique and different page.

—**Mary B. Lucas**, author of *Lunchmeat & Life Lessons: Sharing a Butcher's Wisdom*

Four Ordinary Women is beautifully written. Brutally honest. Funny. Powerful. Comforting. It's impossible to read this book without relating the stories to one's own life - and being moved to treasure some things and to change others.

—**Patricia (Pat) Schudy,** former youth columnist, *Talk to Us,* Universal Press Syndicate

WOW…this was the most powerful, touching, and uplifting piece of reading I have ever read. There are hundreds of books under the heading "Spiritual Reading." This book gives a whole new meaning to the heading…

—**Father Ed Lisson, S.J.**

Four Ordinary Women

Patricia Antonopoulos

Patti Dickinson

Shawna Samuel

Jo Ann Stanley

SEVEN LOCKS PRESS

SANTA ANA, CALIFORNIA

Seven Locks Press
P.O. Box 25689
Santa Ana, CA 92799
(800) 354-5348

Individual sales: This book is available through most bookstores or can be ordered
directly from Seven Locks Press at the address above.

Quantity Sales: Special discounts are available on quantity purchases by corporations,
associations and others. For details, contact the "Special Sales Department" at the
publisher's address above.

Edited by Margery Guest
Cover & Interior Design Kira Fulks • www.kirafulks.com
Printed in the United States of America

Library of Congress Cataloging-in-Publication Data is available from the publisher

ISBN: 978-0-9822293-3-0   0-9822293-3-X

Dedication

The point is this:
that the stream of memory may lead you to the river of understanding.
And understanding, in turn, may be a tributary to the river of forgiveness.
I Know This Much Is True —**Wally Lamb**

For Bob who, by our marriage, welcomed and loved us all.
For the Days of my life.
My children, Mark, Elizabeth, Paul, Dan and Chris
My daughters-in-law, Kaiya (Wolf), Ida and Kristi
My Grandchildren, Cain, Molly, Frank and Sam
Patricia Antonopoulos

To Wood—who has gently encouraged and believed in me and who has been my
good friend for so many years. Together we have raised eight compassionate kids
who have integrity to spare. Thank you for 34 mostly-terrific years
To my kids—Matthew, Elizabeth, Claire, Kathleen, Mary Morgan, Andrew,
Meghan and Margaret – you have changed socks, planes, classes, your underwear,
the channel, your attitude and your mind, but mostly you have changed my life.
I love you all so very much.
Patti Dickinson

To my mom, Sharon,
who put one foot in front of the other during her darkest days—for me.
Shawna Samuel

For my family
Jo Ann Stanley

Acknowledgments

Our thanks to:

James Riordan for taking a second look at our stories
and for believing in what he called the "understated elegance" of
Four Ordinary Women.
He has always been in our corner as publisher, teacher and a friend.

Margery Guest, our editor, who did the difficult work
of sanding the rough edges of our manuscript.

Kira Fulks, who took a box of dog-eared pages
and turned them into the beautiful book we visualized.

Wood Dickinson has been the voice of reason, experience and support throughout
our adventure with *Four Ordinary Women.* He has offered his help in every part of the
process. Because of Wood's input, *Four Ordinary Women* feels completely extra-ordinary.

Bob Antonopoulos stood ready with resources and support
as we worked towards our goals. His voice was quiet, but he never wavered.

Contents:

Four Ordinary Women

Preface

The groundwork for this book was laid in the fall of 1997. It was my son Andrew's first grade year. Mrs. Antonopoulos was his teacher. It would not be stretching the truth to say that she was a legend—passionate about her life's work, teaching with integrity and respect. At the end of that year, she retired to the collective groan of the Westwood View community. Andrew entered second grade, and Mrs. Antonopoulos became his pen pal, and my friend. We shed the cordial, parent/teacher relationship. I was drawn to her ability to express herself gently, to think things through before speaking, her goodness. She was patient, and her eyes sparkled when she smiled. And so over the next three years, our friendship unfolded. She grew into the enormous role she has played in my life—trusted soul mate and companion. We corresponded. We talked of life, its ups and downs. And like a well-worn, comfortable flannel nightgown, we were well-worn, comfortable friends. And that . . . that was the beginning of the book.

In another day, in another time, women could find companionship over the back fence while the children played. Today, women are in many ways isolated from the connectedness that is essential to our existence. Our neighborhoods are NOT the same neighborhoods that we grew up in. Many houses in our neighborhood are empty during the day. Garage door openers insulate us from the weather and, inadvertently, from each other. And so, in January of 2001, Pat and I made some phone calls to see if there was any interest in pulling a group of women together for two hours at Cedar Roe Library's meeting room. Our purpose was to orally share—time was set aside at the beginning of every meeting to express any concerns. Oftentimes this was a crisis that had nothing to do with what we shared in our writing that day. We wrote and ultimately compiled the writing into a book. We began with ten women. It was clear that the writing that we were doing was driving the level of sharing to a deeper, more intimate place. It was really an unexpected result. I suppose that was because the writing forced us all to be more introspective, and to articulate what we REALLY meant. The honing of the words precipitated the honing of the feelings. The quality of the interaction and the connection we felt was profound. Yet the emotional sharing and committing it to paper was gritty work. For several, the potential of publication proved too daunting a risk. The result was the loss of six of the original ten members. Now we were four: JoAnn, Shawna, Pat and Patti. We spoke the unspeakable. We wrote and we wept, individually and collectively. We mourned and we celebrated what was and what wasn't. We offered each other that miraculous gift of acceptance of whatever was spoken, with the promise of confidentiality. It became each woman's prerogative to share writing for inclusion in the book.

Within these pages, you will read the stuff of life—birth and death and the in-between. Marriage, and a runaway kid. Friendship, and what has us looking at the ceiling at three in the morning. This book was written by four ordinary women. Leading ordinary lives.

These women are probably much like you. These stories are all of our stories.

Patti Dickinson
Fairway, Kansas

Invitation Letter of March 2001

Dear,

Share your story, share your insights, and share your strength. You have a unique story or a unique perspective on a universal story. We are paving the way for you to share that story with hundreds of readers.

We believe that the deepening isolation of modern society has diminished the opportunities for personal growth and family stability derived from profound sharing among women. Our goal is to produce a book that will offer a two-fold result: reading the stories will be a substitute for the personal sharing that is so difficult because of our busy schedules; and we want to offer comfort, strength, and hope to readers. The feelings evoked from the stories might encourage women to make the time to develop those friendships that can be so powerful.

We invite and welcome your participation in this group. Please join us. Our first gathering is planned for:

Tuesday, April 17, 2001
at 10:00 a.m.
Cedar Roe Library meeting room.

Join us as we explore our definitions of friendship and support.

If April 17 is not a good time for you, let us know possible dates and times that could fit your schedule. We are anxious to hear from you.

Patricia Antonopoulos
Patti Dickinson

OUR PROMISE OF PRIVACY

OUR PROMISE TO ONE ANOTHER

1. What is said in the group stays in the group.

2. Our pledge of privacy is absolute.

3. Our stories cannot be shared with any other person unless we are physically present or give our specific consent.

4. We are sharing strength and courage.

Biographies in Brief

Getting to Know Us

The events in our lives happen in a sequence in time,
but in their significance to ourselves, they find their own order . . .
the continuous thread of revelation.

—Eudora Welty

Pat Antonopoulos

For 51 years, beginning at age 19, I was defined by perimeters—twice married, once divorced, mother of five, committed Catholic, teacher, grandmother, caregiver, friend, retiree and volunteer.

Not now.

Now I am *becoming*.

I treasure spontaneity and laughter, am impatient with ritual routine, with the mundane. Sitting still, even with a book, is increasingly difficult. Comfort in relationships feels much safer.

Yet, for at least the last five years, I have eaten a whole-wheat bagel each morning, and have worn the *same pair* of Birks each day for those five years. Five pair of jeans and seven denim shirts hang center stage in the closet. Small talk is an art form I have yet to master. Listening is better than talking.

I require a reason for each day, a measure of time and success. The measure is always the people in my life.

This contrast between rigid and free mixes into an annoyingly responsible woman with future plans for singing and dancing.

Patti Dickinson

I was born on the twenty-third day of June in 1953. I married Wood when I was twenty-one, and by twenty-seven had earned the title of "mom." I would repeat that seven more times over the next fourteen years. We would be teased unmercifully by friends who said that we had the market cornered on "front-pew Catholic names": Matt, Elizabeth, Claire, Kathleen, Mary Morgan, Andrew, Meghan and Margaret. Unwavering Irish Catholics.

I feel like I began this motherhood journey thinking I was going to run a 5K and make pretty good time. It has been more like a marathon—alternating between "hitting the wall" and gasping for breath.

My favorite part of parenting is listening to my kids retell stories. Then I am reminded that we've had a riotous good time on many, many occasions. And sometimes, in the day to day, I forget that it hasn't all been lost library books, dead fish, broken curfews, dented fenders, soggy washcloths on the floor of the shower, a sticky refrigerator door handle, or whose turn it is to clean out the bunny cage or the cats' litter box, or to ride in the front seat. That we've celebrated personal and public victories and we've settled our differences and confronted pain in many ways—through tears, slammed doors, quivering chins, stony silences, sobbing, retreating.

My friends would tell you that I am generous, funny, willing to do just about anything for any of them, most likely a stockholder in Gap khaki shorts. My 38 spices are alphabetized but I only use pepper, cinnamon and basil; the rest are for decoration. I am set-your-watch-by-me reliable, always clutching a list of things to do.

My kids would say that I am available, that I know who they are, maybe even when they don't, that I have a big heart, and am a great mom. They say that I am passionate about not incarcerating children, the death penalty, knitting, dimples, honesty, putting their napkins in their laps, mowing every blade of grass—with no residual fringe, curly hair and saying goodnight.

I would tell you that I am sometimes "stuck." Not sure who I am, where I fit. I am estranged from a family that functioned, but sometimes not very well. I am not good at letting much of anything unpleasant run its course, but I enter, stage left, too quickly to fix whatever I perceive to be broken. I am not good with silences—you probably don't want to sit next to me on a cross-country plane trip or stand in front of me to renew your driver's license. I have no fashion sense and carry the same purse until it wears out. (I don't wish I had a fashion sense.) I have a non-existent ability to say no, and I laugh—a lot.

My husband would tell you that I am a morning person, recoil at the mere suggestion of clutter, make a great fried egg sandwich and that sometimes love hurts. That I believe in happy endings and honesty is my guiding principle. That I call it like I see it and don't play games. That I can beat the socks off him in backgammon and it makes him grumpy because I gloat—just a little.

I dedicate my writing to Wood, the man who shared this thirty-year marital journey and to the kids who helped us define ourselves as a family.

Shawna Samuel

Born in 1963, I am a work in progress, always changing, striving to be true to myself and who I want to be. My best friend, my husband Duncan, would probably say that I'm a fun person to be with who has a zest for life he envies. I am innately happy. My glass, and everyone's around me, is full to overflowing. My eternal optimism and passion for doing my best at everything I take on is my mainstay. I have to say I enjoy a great sense of humor. One of my best qualities is that I can laugh at myself and opportunities for this afford themselves daily. While marveling at my multi-tasking and balancing the many activities as mother of two, volunteer and employee, Duncan gets frustrated with my inability to look out for myself, say no now and then, and be my own gatekeeper.

My daughter Caitlin, born in 1988, and son Alex, born in 1995, like and respect me overall, although I can be frustratingly exacting and demanding sometimes. But even as kids, I think they would give me an A + for effort. For even at my worst, they can see that I'm really committed to them and on their side for the long haul.

For my friends, I am loyal, steadfast and supportive. I can keep a secret, listen forever, and come back with some pretty damn good advice now and then. I'm someone you could call at two o'clock in the morning, and you know I wouldn't be mad. I might even make you laugh.

It is both a blessing and a curse that I was born an old soul, wise beyond my years.

Jo Ann Stanley

I'm 52, born in '52: cosmic numbers. I am wife, mother, teacher, learner, and traveler. I use the word "traveler" literally and figuratively. As a young adult—21 on the 21st—I fell in love with travel when I backpacked through South America. This experience largely defined who I am today: it gave me confidence, global awareness, my love of the Spanish language. Since then I've been completely unable to tame my wanderlust. Have passport, will go everywhere! Metaphorically, I am a traveler seeking directions. I find community with friends and family, I care what happens to humanity and the earth, but I'm unclear about my ultimate path.

As lifelong learner, I'm constantly reading. I feel lost when I'm between books, so I'm usually reading several. Inevitably the one I want is in the wrong place: in the car when I'm in the kitchen, in the kitchen when I'm in the car. I'm always looking for things: my book, glasses, or keys.

I am a teacher by vocation. I stumbled into the profession in college, but realize now that it was fate.

Being a teacher has served me well as mother to my two girls, Corinne and Brooke, who have suddenly morphed into teenagers. When they were toddlers, we enjoyed many hours of reading and creativity together. Now they have little use for my teachings if offered unsolicited, but still ask for help now and then.

I'm not exactly a lousy homemaker, but this isn't my forte either. I do love to cook. My darkest secret is my narcolepsy. There I am on the couch, every afternoon, falling asleep with a book in my lap and the cat curled up close. Yet I have a husband—Kerry—who loves me despite my flaws, and in return, he remains the love of my life.

Dear Reader,

Not every story in this book has an ending, nor would each story be the same if written today.

What each chapter does offer is honest sharing from our hearts. This book can hold your hand, walking with you through many moments of your life.

As you read you will know that we honor you, understand your pain, celebrate your triumphs, and share the strength and courage that is yours.

The Authors

PARENTING

What I've learned From My Children

Your children are not your children.
They are the sons, and daughters
of Life's Longing for itself.
They come through you but not from you,
And though they are with you yet they belong not to you.
You may give them your love but not your thoughts,
For they have their own thoughts.

—Kahlil Gibran, *The Prophet*

Patricia Antonopoulos

"In my Father's house, there are many mansions. . ."

My children are such mansions, castles filled with dazzling style and substance.

They are five genetically similar adults with shared experiences. Yet their differences might mark them as strangers.

Each of my children became an adult as he or she processed the values offered, analyzing, matching with his or her reality. Each child discarded any pieces that did not fit the puzzle.

My blessing to them was a sincere desire to honor their reasoning, their intellect, and their truth.

From my children I have learned joy, heartache and heart healing. I have learned that heartache is not heartbreak.

I learned that more was required of me than I knew how to give.

I learned that, to my children, I was a part of their concept of integrity, both from my failures and my successes.

For each of them, I carry both credit and blame. As it should be.

My children are poets and scholars who have both honored and squandered their talents. Their visions often match my own, but just as often, I am blind to what they see.

Each of my children would profess a solid tolerance of people, ideas, and philosophies.

Yet each has boundaries of that tolerance. It is as if they accept wavers in their own sand lines, but have little patience with those who draw more rigid patterns.

A zest for life, a need for adrenaline, a spirit of adventure are all joys shared by my children. They play with passion.

From their diversity, I have learned greater tolerance, acceptance, and understanding.

Their ongoing gift to me is the unshakeable knowledge that I must be vigilant as I attempt to walk the walk.

Patti Dickinson

That vanilla ice cream with black specks is the best flavor.

That sometimes the littlest Dickinson sister has the inside skinny on what is really going on around here. Standing outside the bathroom door while her eleven-year-old brother runs the water in the sink, gets his hair wet (no soap, she said) and comes out, claiming to have SHOWERED. All this just from listening at the door. Is she good or what?

That ketchup should be red. Not purple. Not green.

That in the wee hours of Christmas Eve, when the kids are asleep, the stockings drooping from their hangers and just the little white lights of the tree lit in the living room, it really is a silent and holy night.

That even on the worst of days, I still look at at least one kid and think, "Where have the years gone?"

That some amazing communication can happen on a walk through the neighborhood in the dark with only one kid.

That no matter how convincing a kid is about how they will take care of the cat, fish, and/or bunny if you get it for them, it will be the mom (never the dad or the kid who did the begging and promising) who gets out of bed every night, after she has already gotten IN bed, to check and see if the pets have food, flakes or hay. They won't.

That it is possible to have two broken collar bones on two different kids AND a broken leg within a year and NOT have Social and Rehabilitation Services ringing the doorbell.

That I think that taking a forgotten ham sandwich to school (kid made) with a mom note inside is part of my job description (some people would say that doing that deprives kids of the opportunity to learn responsibility—I think my kids will still file an income tax return when they are adults, even if they have to file an extension).

That there is nothing more naturally beautiful than a kid who's spent the day at the beach—sunburned and sand-sprinkled.

That hope and courage are two qualities you can't have too much of when you're a mom.

That it is even better if hope and courage are dad qualities too.

That an adult's and a kid's definition of music that is too loud, trash that needs emptying, a room that needs cleaning or a car that needs washing are not the same.

That kids don't get rickets or become metabolically out of balance if they have cereal for dinner once in a while.

That newborns are warm and smell—well, like newborns, but even middle school and high school kids like to be surprised with a headlock and have their hair ruffled.

That thunderstorms and snowstorms are wonderful incentives to gather together in the same room of the house.

That a baby beginning to fuss in the middle of the night will NEVER just go back to sleep, so you may as well just get up.

That if you haven't laid awake worrying about something kid-related in the last month, you're probably doing too much yoga or need to check for a pulse.

Shawna Samuel

*W*hat a journey! I've gone from being a single woman, to a married professional to a stay-at-home mom of one, and then two. I have learned a great deal along the way. Mostly, I feel lucky to have been able to take this path. I've not only learned from the experience, but I've become a totally different person. I grew up with a task before me to accomplish. I worked hard, generally accomplished my goals, and moved on. I constantly set perfectionist ideals for myself. Then. . . I had children. Being a mother doesn't offer a pay scale, award certificates or goal setting sessions of the professional world, and it is mutually exclusive to perfectionism. I was a great parent until I actually became one. It can feel like a dark abyss of fuzzy demands and constantly changing challenges.

I learned that raising children is not a task you complete. It goes on and on and constantly challenges you in ways you never imagined. The emotions involved are stronger than any I have ever experienced. Challenges can be large or small, such as answering questions on the way into the grocery store like, "Does God have bones? Why don't aliens have hair? What's inside the sun that makes it so hot?" Or after picking out brown eggs, "Are these ones chocolate inside?"

You can feel pride that your kindergartner is walking confidently into class, not even turning to wave goodbye, but, at the same time, heart stabbing pain at letting go. Or it can just as easily be the opposite, peeling a crying child off your leg at preschool, turning quickly, and walking confidently away, turning a cold back, but not a cold heart. Which hurts more? Both are sharp. But what other experience could offer so much pain, yet be so rewarding? It is the love for them that carries you on and helps you meet, if not conquer, each challenge.

I've learned that the challenges are not static. They transform daily, almost hourly. You must be flexible to stand a chance of keeping up and staying sane. The polar extremes you can face each day as a parent are vast. I heard once that raising your kids goes by so quickly; it's just those days and nights that are so damn long. So true. I remember days with newborns where I didn't think I could make it until 5 o'clock much less until they were 18. But there could be moments within those challenging days that I never wanted to end, like holding a sleeping baby because it was so joyful, not because I had to. Or when my two-year-old would come down for the morning and announce, "Hey, it's day now. I found it upstairs!"

Having a family has brought out the best in me, and the worst. I've learned who I am when I'm at the end of my rope. I've also learned, when my head's on straight, how powerfully I can love, guide, and teach right from wrong, good from bad. You can mold children's images of themselves as easily as if you had Play-Doh in your hands. I've learned how vulnerable children are, and how it's the little things, little words or actions that mean so much to them, that shape them and their feelings about the world, themselves, and you.

I've learned that tough definitely has a place in the same sentence with love, and that while I can be a softy, barely able to muster the courage to be firm sometimes, at other times, I can easily come across tougher than I have to be without effort. But children do grow up, whether we win parenting awards or not. All parents start out thinking that they will be the perfect parent, that they will not make mistakes, that they can't make mistakes because the stakes are too high. But this is so untrue. Mistakes are made by the bushel, but it is the effort and love behind trying and never giving up that counts.

Having young children forces you to slow down, enjoy the simple pleasures, and learn about the world all over again. Going on slow walks together and discovering the outdoors again is wonderful. "Hey, butterfly begins with butter!" may be the discovery of the day. Or, "You know, Panda bears look like soccer balls!" Or learning colors over some flowers when your toddler says, "This one's a trixie one!" And how about enjoying a popsicle again? "This one's strawberry, this one's blueberry, this one's. . . yellowberry; this one's greenberry. . ." Knowing that your child is beginning to learn right from wrong can become rewardingly clear at an early age when, after you run to the sound of a crying child, your son says, "He just fell going up the steps with nobody doin' stuff." Mission accomplished, at least for this day.

More than anything, I suppose, with children's growing bodies and phases blatantly marking the quick passage of time, I've learned that all you are given for sure is this moment, and this day. Having a family has taught me to live each day to the fullest, a theory that sometimes seems foolish when a day is spent doing laundry, cooking and cleaning. But that's simply what we're given each day. I've learned to feel blessed and grateful to have that. As Mother Theresa said, "Sometimes you can't do great things, only small things with great love." For me, making that realization is the greatest gift of all.

Jo Ann Stanley

From whispery afternoons spent nursing my baby girl came a calm I never knew before. When she fell asleep I laid her down in her white wicker bassinet with pink and white coverlet—not knowing then that the soft square of fabric had a name: "Blankey." In the evening I practiced mind over madness when the colic came and she cried and cried. Patience not proving sufficient, I turned to more desperate measures, placing her seat on the dryer to vibrate, driving with no destination, vacuuming a clean rug with baby in snuggly. Finally Daddy came home and held her, the little belly down on his forearm, tiny head cradled in his palm, and he sang his lullabies to this awkward appendage while I managed to put food on the table. Very soon I learned that night was not all that different from day—though it was dark.

Then came the pattering of toddlers in footed pajamas. I realized now that a walk around the block could easily consume an hour, what with acorn distractions and colored leafy detours. I learned to slow my pace, to recover the wonder of discovery. At home I learned that anytime might be teatime, that those plastic cups and saucers demanded an animate and animated guest each time they came out of the basket, not to mention the doctor's kit requiring a patient, the choo-choo its engineer, the stuffed dog its woof. Those queens and princesses draped in my old lingerie were haughty, imperious. So I fawned. When pretend grew boring and we wanted projects, I learned how to make kaleidoscopes out of paper towel tubes, necklaces of painted pasta, Play-Doh of flour. My creativity soared.

Along the way I learned what was important. It wasn't me, it was them. I learned about unconditional love. My children were not always what I wanted them to be, but I loved them anyway. Nature is what the children bring to us; nurture is what we bring to them.

School, homework, parent-teacher conferences. Thank goodness my husband could do geometry. Make-up, tight clothing, and hip-hop. BOYFRIENDS! I always felt comfortable as mother to two girls, until now. If I fail any parenting exam, it will be the one on adolescence.

The lessons learned from family life are ongoing, more like a never-ending tutorial than a finite semester. Fortunately there are progress reports: a first tooth, a graduation, or a daughter's wedding day. Still there is never an end to the course, never a fixed grade, and the only diploma one receives reads like a bumper sticker: HAD C-SECTION, SCARRED FOR LIFE.

INSPIRATIONS AND INFLUENCES

Who Drew the Face of Me?

The greatest masterpieces were once only pigments on a palette.

—Henry Haskins

Patricia Antonopoulos

Approaching the evening hours of life is a good time to examine the bits and pieces as they rearrange yet again. As with any life, there have been bitter mists to bind the spirit, and shudder the heart. Yet the victory is always with the sunrise.

Maybe I allowed myself to become the warden of my life, stringing razor wire across feelings that threatened to consume. Always, gloriously always, I have been rescued—by a word, a look, a moment, a flick of nature, a sound, a melody, a friendship—something made the old new again.

Harper Lee held that pencil to my portrait. Atticus Finch was, and is, my definition of integrity. Robin William's character in *Dead Poets Society* and Richard Dreyfus in *Mr. Holland's Opus* gave some depth to my teaching. I loved books like *Winter Wheat*, by Mildred Walker, where the heroine could stand alone, living by principle, needing only the affirmation of her own beliefs.

My five children have taught me more about life than I could have imagined before their existence. The old cliché about a parent getting smarter as the children get older is reversed. I have shared in their wisdom as they have grown and I have matured.

Twelve years of Catholic education helped me find a center that has never wavered, even though I was away from that church for a time. My sister, Susan, and I attended daily Mass from second grade through two years of college. Walking together in first light, season after season, was a cherished experience. We believed with conviction and innocence.

I loved school—the buildings, the teachers, the structure and traditions, the discipline, the challenges. Walking home at noon to fix lunch for my siblings, cleaning the kitchen, starting the preparations for dinner was my time to appreciate responsibility. Finding a few moments to read—to visit Manderley, to become the second Mrs. De Winter, loving Maxim, and fearing Mrs. Danvers was my ritual escape into fantasy.

Friends and people encountered in passing have helped me draw the face of the woman I want to be, to become. Friends from years ago, forgotten names and faces gave me bits and pieces. True and honest friends, known and cherished today, give me their strength and courage. Friends who listen and are not distracted help me discover ideas that would not have been my own.

Time alone, walking, skating, jogging, is a time for the unearned gift of insight. Without effort, the sorting—the inspirations—come during these hours of physical activity.

Music waylays my emotions, not to be trusted for inspiration alone. Music can crumble my resolve, search out a hidden emotion, and influence every part of my life.

Perhaps those are not lines and wrinkles reflected from the mirror. Perhaps they are the outlines created of those bits and pieces of experiences. Perhaps each line is a marker for time treasured with the people of my life.

Now that is something old made new again!

Patti Dickinson

My dad gave me a work ethic, and a sense of humor.

Sister Nordmann taught me that telling the truth allows you to live with yourself. That's when caught red-handed, after a quick senior year cigarette or two in a friend's car in the parking lot, I came into school in a cloud of Marlboro-smoke, and she asked the inevitable question of my friend and me. Instead of making an overblown example of us, we talked quietly in her office, and it stopped there.

My grandmother taught me that I had value *just because* and her trudge up the hill to St. Brendan's every Sunday was a teachable moment for me—a lesson in humble faith, in perseverance, in quiet leadership.

Miss Cramarus is the reason I majored in English, and is responsible for the amount of money I spend at Border's. She showed me perhaps the first model of the village—overstepping the traditional parameters of her job in the classroom. We spent many Saturday mornings together in her apartment, talking about books and life when I was the newly transplanted kid from Kansas City, in a new school and had no moorings to attach to yet.

My first college roommate taught me that it is possible to survive living with another human being, and that not everyone is a morning person. Specifically this was drummed into me every single morning as I brushed my teeth at the sink, as she would shriek in martyred, irrational irritation from beneath the covers, "DO YOU HAVE TO BRUSH YOUR TEETH SO LOUD?" I got even by closing the door behind me louder than was necessary as I left our dorm room. More than a handful of times.

Jim Rubino, a therapist friend, taught me that I was not put on this earth to be the General Manager of the Universe. God already is gainfully employed doing that.

A college friend's parents showed me a model of a family dinner table that I still use today, minus the three kinds of pie. Laughter, camaraderie, acceptance, sharing the day. These were simple, generous farm people who owned a small turkey farm in the hill country of Austin, Texas.

My mom taught me to put on that public face, and to smile. Just smile.

The Kansas City Star editorial page editor taught me that I had opinions worthy of a public forum and that writing passionate letters to the editor was nearly addictive.

My kids taught me that I love every single stage. That I have enjoyed 99.6 percent of watching them evolve into who they are, and who they are becoming. They have shown me that I can endure, appreciate and agonize, give and talk until I'm blue in the face. That I have within me the full capacity of emotions.

My two oldest kids have taught me humility and finding new ways to love.

My spouse taught me that being best friends is a damn good way to begin a marriage, that an apology, spoken from the heart, can mend just about anything and that an attentive companion to hash things over with is one of life's best gifts.

Shawna Samuel

Veta. My sweet grandmother Veta drew the face of me. And I'm lucky that she did. She is a woman who never accomplished what you could say were great, huge things in her life. She lived an ordinary life. But I absorbed who she was. She was very different than my mother. She provided a new dimension in my life. My mother and I both struggled with perfection.

Veta, God love her, was far from a perfectionist. She always made do with what she had. Her house was comfortable, but nothing out of a magazine. Mostly, I always felt safe and relaxed there. Veta was a woman who enjoyed the process of life, not just the results. As an awkward, clumsy kid, I could spill, break and plunder, and Veta never minded. She let me play with her good china set to have a tea party, and her best jewelry to play dress up. I apparently hooked all of the jewelry clasps in her carpet, and yanked to free them until both the jewelry and the carpet were ruined. She didn't care. She never once raised her voice to me. I was more important to her than the jewelry and carpet put together. She would garden to feel the dirt in her hands and let a little seed have a chance rather than for the result of the flower at the end. She never purchased an animal in her life, but strays always found her, and she was never without cats and dogs.

Granted, it's easier to be a grandparent than a parent without the crushing responsibilities of raising a child. Maybe that's why God invented grandparents. But I know that if I'd not had that warm, unconditionally accepting and non-judgmental voice of Veta in my head, I would not have been able to fight the expectations that I set for myself as a child. She is always in my heart telling me it's OK just to be me.

Jo Ann Stanley

Who drew the face of me? Other than my parents, the person who has had the greatest influence on my life is my aunt, Helen Morgan, an amazing woman to whom I must pay tribute.

When I was a little girl, Helen represented everything exotic and adventurous. She was a woman ahead of her time: divorced, independent, intellectual. She spoke many languages: Latin, French, Spanish, Russian. Aunt Helen sailed for Turkey the year I was born, as a missionary for the United Church of Christ. Her job was teaching English at a boarding school for girls. We have wonderful photographs of her leaving from New York Harbor, waving from the crowded deck of a huge ship. Her letters home soon told of minarets and mosques, the call to prayer, the sultan's palace, the Bosporus and the bazaar. She learned yet another language: Turkish.

Every seven years, Helen came home to Washington, D.C. on furlough. She traveled the U.S. giving slide show talks about Turkey in churches across the land, raising funds. Yet she made time for family, and she took each of her nieces and nephews on a private excursion. I remember so well my special day with Aunt Helen. I was six years old with a horrible pixie haircut, outrageous freckles, a chipped front tooth and my best pink dress. We rode the trolley into downtown Washington and visited a mosque, a kind of church I had never seen before, where people took their shoes off and prayed on the floor. We had lunch in Woody's, a fancy department store, and went to a Smithsonian museum, where she purchased for me a Chinese parasol, my most prized possession throughout childhood.

Soon after, I began my lifelong correspondence with Aunt Helen. I was in first grade, just learning to write. She has saved those childish letters, has them still at 91 years of age, after 26 years in Turkey, 2 trips around the world, and 25 years in California. My mother saved all of Helen's beautiful letters home, and I saved my foreign doll collection. I still have the dolls Helen gave me from Japan, China, Europe, Thailand, and of course, Turkey.

When I was thirteen, Helen came home on furlough again. I borrowed her Turkish phrase book and decided to self-teach Turkish. To make everything more challenging, I simultaneously decided to learn Hebrew because my best friend at the time was Jewish. It was a doomed process, what with foreign alphabets and guttural, twisted pronunciations. My mind became hopelessly muddled and I bogged down.

In my twenties, I was fortunate to have the opportunity to visit Helen at her school, the American Kiz Lisesi in Uskudar, Turkey. The campus of this all girls' boarding school was then a short ferry ride across the Bosporus from Istanbul. On a sunny day, when the water sparkles, there is nothing more glorious than being in a boat as it crosses the Bosporus Straits! Today Helen's school is coeducational, and a huge bridge over the Bosporus connects the continents of Europe and Asia. Helen tells a story of standing on the bridge the day it opened. Because so many people were on the structure at once, it began to shake and there was a panic, a stampede.

During the visit with Helen, I had many wonderful experiences: we bargained in the bazaar and toured the Sultan's palace and we visited the ruins of Troy. We watched a performance of Turkish folkdance at the school, and I attempted to make lasagna in a country that does not sell lasagna noodles. I ended up making homemade noodles for the first and only time in my life, a near disaster. Each afternoon we attended the faculty tea, and I met many of Helen's dearest friends and colleagues. One day a wealthy associate of Helen's, one of her donor parents, sent his chauffeur to drive my friend and me north along the Bosporus to the Black Sea; in the village there we purchased delicate blouses with blue embroidery. Later we traveled inland to view the strange rocks and caves of Cappadocia, a landscape like that of the moon. Probably because of Helen, I crave travel and new frontiers, and like her I have wandered the globe to an unusual degree.

Helen was a missionary, but the Turkish government prohibits any proselytizing by Christians. In essence, Helen was an educator. She taught English for one year at the school before being promoted to principal. In her tenure as principal she had many achievements; there's even a building named after her: the Morgan Hall of Science and Technology. But Helen remains proudest of her graduates. A number of them have been lifelong friends. This is true also of Helen's colleagues from those years. Like Helen, I became an English and Spanish teacher. I never did get anywhere with Turkish, though. When I think of my accomplishments, I try to think first of any progress made by my children or my students.

After Helen returned to the United States, she moved to California where she now lives in retirement. After my mom and my husband's mom died, both in the same year, Helen became a grandmother to my kids. She crocheted blankets for each of them when they were still in their cribs. She came to our home every Christmas. On visits, Aunt Helen fascinated my girls with her stories, her piano playing, and most especially with her talent for creating ribbon fish. Helen always brought along her ribbon kit: small scissors, spools of ribbon in a rainbow of colors, nearly invisible fishing line, and Avery dots for eyeballs. After asking for a child's choice of colors, she deftly wove the glossy strips into a delicate fish, ready to hang on the Christmas tree. I tried to learn how to make these beautiful fish but never could, although my daughter Brooke has mastered it and will carry forward that tradition. Now that Helen can no longer travel to our home, we visit her in California whenever we can. I have become fond of her unique community, Pilgrim Place, and the loving individuals who reside there.

All of her life, Helen was a writer. Helen has given our family many unusual gifts garnered from her travels: the Turkish plates displayed in the dining room, the statues of whirling dervishes that twirl on the piano, a Chinese bell for Corinne, a statue of a Chinese god for Brooke. But Helen's greatest gifts to the family are her own letters and journals, which both fascinate and inspire. I'd like to be a writer as gifted as Helen: I'd like to write a book about her, about her childhood in Chicago during the depression, her years at the University of Chicago, her year as a translator of Russian for the US government, her tenure as a Spanish professor at Macalister College, her life in Turkey, her worldwide travels, her wit, her brilliance, and her faith. Helen always wanted to write her memoirs. I hope my sister and I can do this for her, editing her letters, telling her story, as she has given us so much.

It fills my heart to know that Helen has been a source of great influence and inspiration not only to me, but to my sister, to my daughters, and to hundreds of young girls in a country far away from here.

I close with a poem my daughter wrote after a visit to Helen in California. Corinne was eleven years old and studying French at the time:

> Helen, 0 Helen, we love you well,
> Helen, 0 Helen, of the Chi-nese Bell,
> Helen, 0 Helen, we now bid you good-bye
> Helen, 0 Helen, we leave with a sigh.

—Chantal

SPIRITUAL BELIEFS

Soul-Searching

The opposite of love is not hate, it's indifference.
The opposite of art is not ugliness, it's indifference.
The opposite of faith is not heresy, it's indifference.
The opposite of life is not death, it's indifference.

—Elie Wiesel

Patricia Antonopoulos

In his book, *Nickel Mountain*, John Gardner wrote a few paragraphs that inadvertently matched my search for spiritual beliefs. A character in the book read the daily paper, column by column, page by page, front to back. This character read with intensity, never leaving a page until each word, first to last, was read. If a story were begun on page 1 and completed on page 10, he did not reach the ending until he had read pages 1 through 9. A great deal of information interfered between beginning and ending.

Before I was a week old, I was baptized in the Catholic Church, which I now attend. I believe in the sanctuary of a church, in the value and comfort of tradition and ritual. I strongly believe in the need for a church community to help us persist in the good. I believe that unless a value system permeates every facet of life, it is a false system. I believe that accepting evil is easier than persisting in good.

During my life, I have searched, looking again and again, mentally begging my church to be enough. It was enough through high school.

During the Catholic Mass, we recite a prayer of forgiveness. We ask forgiveness "... for what I have done and what I have failed to do."

It is my belief that what I have failed to do has the greater need for forgiveness.

Time, culture, need, and circumstance directed the drawing of a Supreme Being, a knowable God.

The Bible, the Torah, and the Koran are powerful books, often reinterpreted to fit the needs of time and culture.

Paul's letter to the Corinthians (12, 31-13, 8) and the Sermon on the Mount containing the Eight Beatitudes might have been enough.

The 21st century does not need multiplied loaves and fishes, or water into wine. Our visible miracles are those of science and medicine. The miracle we need is a cleansing of our minds and morality.

Defining immorality feels impossible. Deliberate and evil is as close as I can come. Defining evil polarizes the most honest of intentions.

The Book of Genesis contains the Christian belief that man was created in the image and likeness of God. Further into the Bible, we are admonished, "Judge not lest you be judged." I struggle with this. I struggle as I search for the definition of evil, with finding that line that defines evil, and requires judgment.

Judgment persists, even though a strong Christian belief is said to honor, ". . . in the image and likeness of God."

History proves this reality of constant judgment, severe condemnation and a belief in the right to judge.

I believe that all manner of wondrous good is in humanity. Good exists to the extent that human beings can persist.

Goodness has a huge disadvantage. To remain good, rules must be followed.

Evil has no rules. Evil exists to the degree humans allow.

Patti Dickinson

I am a cradle-Catholic. I am a product of a Catholic education, elementary and high school. I grew up in a Catholic home—but a home that wasn't comfortable with the dialogue of our Catholic faith. It was pretty much what we were on Sundays. Both my grandmothers, however, were devout Catholics. Holy cards and rosary beads. I wore a scapular, and read *The Lives of the Saints* over and over and over by flashlight. Thought perhaps, at one point that I would make a pretty good martyr. I longed to be the May Queen. Never happened. I went to college and took a sabbatical from Catholicism until my junior year. Sitting in the dorm on a Saturday night with a friend (who later joined the Sisters of Saint Joseph) and she said, "Hey, let's go to Midnight Mass at the Catholic Student Center. There's this incredible priest, Father Moser." So I said, "How do we know HE'LL be saying Mass?" (After all, how bad would it be to go to Mass and waste forty-five minutes if a dud priest said Mass?) "We'll call." So I called. I said to the male voice that answered the phone at eleven p.m., "Can you tell me who's saying Mass tonight?" in much the same way you'd call a diner to find out what the early bird special was. He said, "I am—I'm Father Moser. Would you do me a favor?" "Sure." "If you decide to come, would you introduce yourself to me after Mass? I'd really like to meet you." I introduced myself, and he married Wood and I two years later. We joked about that scenario many, many times—me, the girl in overalls returning to the church.

I believe in God. It's where I turn when everything is crumbling around me. It's what explains the orange, crimson and yellow pallet of the leaves turning in the fall, and the seashells in the sand on the shores of Cape Cod. It's the miracle of conception, the being-in-the-right-place-at-the-right-time to adopt three kids. It's who I raged at with each of three miscarriages. It's who I implored in the still of the night when Elizabeth ran away. "What's the message here, God? What's the message?" Like in this world, there is a director. There is a choreography to this thing called a lifetime. It's what I call, God-writing-straight-with-crooked-lines.

There are many Catholic tenets that I have trouble with. Still, I never considered changing religions, because the Mass, the tradition of the Catholic Church is probably in my DNA. I believe in the sanctity of life. I am opposed to the death penalty. I believe that priests should be allowed to marry. I'm not too sure about the Pope's infallibility. I'm not sure it matters. I just know that the Mass, the Stations of the Cross, the music, and receiving Communion touch something deep inside me. They reach my core.

One of my biggest problems with the Catholic Church is that those of us raised in this religion were not encouraged to question, to think through things for ourselves. There is a very clear-cut set of rules, many of which are inflexible, rigid. Birth control is wrong. Never right. Try telling THAT to a family that cannot take on the burden of one more baby. The Catholic religion sees many things in just black and white, and perhaps the world is better viewed in shades of gray. Missing Mass on Sunday is considered a mortal sin. So is murder. Robbing a bank. Come on. Yet, in seeming contradiction, this is one of the things I like most about the Catholic Church. We've not watered things down, nor lowered the bar. We know what we stand for.

I guess my spiritual beliefs are felt. Maybe not yet ready to be defined with words.

Shawna Samuel

I was baptized and confirmed an Episcopalian and seamlessly married an Episcopalian. While I've always been immersed in the Christian faith, I have interest and respect for all other religions. I once dated a Jewish boy, and while it was never serious, I found his faith fascinating and full. I am comfortable in the Episcopal Church. The services are nearly as formal as Catholic services, and I love the pomp and circumstance. The rituals, repeated prayers and music are all important parts of my worship experience.

Having very little formal Christian education, I feel out of my element when discussing specifics of the Bible. Sometimes I feel like a cheater, an imposter. I have never read the whole Bible, and don't know most of the stories and lessons. I have merely skimmed the surface, I am ashamed to admit. My family did not attend church when I was little, so I never went to Sunday school. I did go through a 6-week confirmation class at age 12, but that's it.

So the fundamentals and details of being an Episcopalian can be quite beyond me. But my feeling of faith, my belief in knowing that there is a God is very strong. I believe in fate, that there is a bigger picture, that life will take the general course it is meant to take. My eternal optimism plays into this nicely. I feel the presence of God, and believe in the power of prayer. When Duncan broke his leg, and it wasn't healing well, we asked for prayers, even from people that we didn't know. From that moment on, Duncan improved. I am convinced that prayer played a role.

My vision of heaven is vague. I don't have the stereotypical picture of it as walking on clouds in white robes with winged angels flitting about, but I believe in the warm, comforting light that people have claimed to see while dying. I believe that we will be reunited with those who have died before us. I have wondered about reincarnation, and believe that it is possible; but haven't really worked it all out in my mind. I am not afraid of dying. I don't think that this life is all there is.

When my grandfather was dying, he was already removed from this world and unresponsive to all of us with eyes glazed over. It was much like watching a machine slow down and finally stop. Right before he quit breathing, he opened his eyes, looked up in the comer of the room, and smiled the most joyful, euphoric smile I had ever seen. His eyes were filled with peace, and he was gone. The nurse opened the window, to let his soul go out. I felt sadness for me, but relief for him.

I trust in whatever lies ahead for us all. I trust there is a greater power, in whatever form. And I believe none are excluded from this greatness. When the world seems cruel and rough, my faith is always what I turn to for comfort.

Jo Ann Stanley

I believe that faith is one of the strongest human powers. History tells how the faith of one teenaged girl who heard voices made separate nations of England and France. Faith brought one woman to India where she fed and ministered to thousands of the sick and dying in the streets of Calcutta. As it has been written, faith can move mountains.

Despite my desire for faith, I find I do not have any. Religion eludes me. Further, I question the role of religion in history and politics. How many wars have been fought in the name of one god or another? How much hate have religious differences generated? In today's world, how many people continue to be divided over questions of faith? For me, organized religion has failed to exemplify morality. My sense of right and wrong has more to do with ideals of empathy, tolerance, and kindness.

I find it much easier to believe in science. When I visited the Galapagos Islands, I was in awe of Charles Darwin. The iguanas there look like little dinosaurs; as he observed, the planet appears younger there, still in the throes of volcanic change. The animals, having developed in isolation from the mainland, have no innate fear of humankind. Birds land close at hand. Some of the creatures seen there exist nowhere else on earth. Have you ever seen a blue-footed booby? As I traveled from island to island, I witnessed the adaptations made by giant Galapagos turtles. On one island, where they had to reach for the leaves that fed them, they had long necks. In another place, their necks were short because food was close to the ground. After visiting these magical isles, it is impossible for me disregard evolutionary theory as some fundamentalists do.

But of course, not all Christians are literal creationists. Many people who believe in evolution and science also believe in God and the Garden of Eden. They can accept the miracles of creation and Christ via faith. This is the piece that I'm missing. I was raised and confirmed in the United Church of Christ, but never completely convinced that it wasn't all hogwash. Today, when I go to church, as I occasionally do, I feel comforted by the sense of community and by the familiar cadences of the minister's voice. I enjoy the warmth of ceremony, the acolytes lighting the candles, the flowers decorating the altar. I love the music, both the music performed and the joy of singing in a group. But I cannot accept the mythology. I feel like a hypocrite when in church, because I just don't believe in the story. To me, Jesus was a person and a prophet. I believe he existed historically. But I can't buy the Immaculate Conception, and I have doubts about the promise of life after death. It seems more self-evident that we rot in the ground. I am fully prepared to be cremated in order to hasten the process of returning to nature.

I do feel awe in the presence of nature. A snow-capped mountain, a field of purple lupine, a deer running in the meadow, these visions cause me to catch my breath in my throat and to wonder at such extreme beauty. Is this God? And often there are times that I feel a spiritual closeness with those that have died, a strong sense of my mother's presence, or my father's guiding hand, or my friend Ron's voice in my ear, but I cannot say whether they speak to me from another realm or whether it's simply a trick of memory and emotion, a psychological phenomenon. So I cannot completely discredit the notion of a god, or of another plane of existence. But neither am I convinced of it.

I am still seeking faith, but at this point in my life I fear I may be too cynical to ever find it: I do envy those of you who have faith: I see how it inspires, how it anchors, how it comforts, how it answers some of life's more difficult questions. Because our family rarely attends church, I sometimes wonder if I am cheating my children of certain chances and choices. The Sunday school stories and church traditions that were a part of my background have not been available to them. Yet at the same time, I believe my husband and I have helped them to develop strong values and moral conduct. So I have to trust that as they mature, they will find their own spiritual views.

The Yardstick
of our Becoming

Perfection has one grave defect: it is apt to be dull.

—W. Somerset Maugham

Patricia Antonopoulos

Once upon a time . . . that fairy tale beginning with a happily ever after tag. More like one step forward, two steps back.

Too many days slip by with little focus on moral growth, too much focus on not growing wider.

This topic won't write for me. I have tried. A two-page Personal Growth sermonette that sounds politically correct via self-help books is printed and perched atop the wastebasket. It belongs inside that trash container.

Change doesn't follow knowledge with ease. Maybe I know how to mend a relationship, but the doing is the growing.

Just when I think I have grown, changed to come closer to the self I want, the thing happens. The slip-back thing, the revert thing, back to old reactions instead of acting on the new me rehearsed so often in my mind.

And there is this aging thing that makes the status quo seem like a labor up the hill. How can I grow when I cannot remember which toothbrush, red or blue, is for the morning?

The Fairy Godmother can whisk that wand and tatters turn to treasure. I want that. I want my tatters into truth, growth, success in finding my voice, my honest and complete self.

And I am trying.

Patti Dickinson

Many, many false starts on this assignment. I sat down at the kitchen table Tuesday morning—with the beginnings of worry etching away at my stomach lining—four cups of coffee into the morning. Better than three weeks to complete this assignment, and I'm down to the last forty-eight hours. Before I can connect pencil to paper, Margaret makes three attempts to begin conversation, "How many more days till the Christmas Program?" "Six." "Did you know how to make a heart—you make an M, and then make the ends of the M's into a point at the bottom." "Wow." "Did you know that the green M & M's have faces on them now?" Sigh.

Can't get the traction I need to get going. I can't seem to find a starting point for this rambling that I know will help me define the growth. But for now, nothing. I KNOW I've grown. These last two years have stretched me—the physical stress of a houseful of little kids has given way, seemingly overnight, to the mental stress of teenagers. Car seats, chicken pox and cabin fever have been replaced by curfews, control and cars.

Growth is measured not by inches, but by attitude, outlook. It is about incremental adjustments in how I view things. A new awareness of just how many shades of gray life has. The past year has been a roller coaster ride with my two oldest kids. Out of that wreckage has come sadness, profound and paralyzing. Out of that has come the realization that I wasn't too good at grieving. Sadness is a noun. Grieving is a verb. I guess I'm better at nouns. Some of the growth is ridiculous—I go out of my way to smile at kids with non-traditional hair colors—I am grateful that our stint with Elizabeth's black hair with red tips is done. But I know that some adult in the outdoor program in Oregon not only smiled at my kid, but looked beyond the hair color to the heart and soul that is her essence and repackaged her and sent her home. Some nameless/faceless someone unconditionally accepted my kid with all her baggage and attitude and saw something in her that I couldn't, wouldn't, was too angry to. My smiles to Crayola-haired teens is a way to pay it forward.

I haven't found my footing yet where Matt is concerned. I'm still searching for a way to walk through, not around, that grief.

I think that there was a turning point, a certain resignation. Reaching out in our gatherings was a way to admit that the pain was no longer bearable as a solo activity—that the comfort of women friends, who were gently honest and whose compassion and empathy was something I could get my arms around. Such a lifeline. It was here that I could admit that the steady/sturdy thing just wasn't working, that my spouse and I were coping and grieving differently, out of sync. It was a moment of such honesty. It was a way of embracing my real life, not some ideal life. And real life means releasing the "could have been's", and "if only's" and dealing with what is. (See paragraph one for what is.) And that is probably where the defining moment happened in my personal growth.

Still much growing to do. Those timeworn tapes that we all have in our heads. I have one that says, "The measure of the mom is her kids." Intellectually I know that isn't so. And I don't measure any other mom that way. Yet that is a standard, a yardstick that I cannot put aside. I know that at some point, to be emotionally healthy, I will need to address that—why the big failures of my kids are MY failures. Seems like a huge can of worms at this point.

Shawna Samuel

The three years from age 23 to 26 were phenomenal for me. During those years, I married, became a homeowner, had an active, challenging and exciting career, gave birth to our first daughter Caitlin, retired and became a full-time mom.

But when I think about who I was then, and who I am now at 41, I have to say that the time of most personal growth has been during the last three years. When I look at my life and the challenges I have faced, the last three years have been the most uneventful. However, I continue to grow and develop in important ways every day. I learn from everything I am involved in. I have so many balls up in the air today, yet feel I handle it all with much more maturity and grace than I ever could have in my 20s. I am more aware of my strengths and weaknesses, of where I want my life to go.

For instance, I'm able to speak my mind, on the spot, when the occasion requires it. At a recent city council meeting with 30 in attendance, including news reporters, not only was I able to stand up to an imposing figure, but I didn't blush from here to Nebraska. In a neighbor relationship that is taxing, sometimes daily, I am able to speak my mind in a fair and even way, and feel better for it, not worse. And with my mother I'm finally able to share feelings that might cause conflict in a constructive, not hurtful way. I am light years ahead of where I was a decade ago.

I consider us all works in progress. I see infinite room in myself for growth, improvement and change. My greatest wish is that at age 80, my answer to the question, "What three-year period shows the most personal growth and change?" my answer will still be, "The last three."

Jo Ann Stanley

The time is NOW. I've never felt more self-actualized, more aware of my creative self, my talents and my limitations. I've never before understood myself so well. I've never understood my past until now. I've never been happier. The various threads of my life are all twisting together to form a thick string.

At one time in my life, my interests and friends seemed much more compartmentalized. There were people I could confide in and others with whom I was more guarded. I wasn't always completely myself. Now I find I have more confidence. I'm more likely to say what I think. I've become more comfortable with who I am. I've become not only a self-advocate but an advocate for my children. I'm happy in my marriage and proud of my girls who are emerging as women. As I move toward a stronger sense of myself within and beyond my family, I find that once different parts of my life are blending together in a beautiful way.

For example, I've always loved words, loved language. I enjoy games like Scrabble, Perquacky, and Fictionary. I studied French, then Spanish, and English, always English. I love reading, I love Shakespeare, I love drama, fiction, and memoir. I love teaching about words, loved teaching English literature and now I enjoy teaching Spanish. The fact that this year I began a new job teaching Spanish in my local elementary school brings together my lifelong love of languages, my joy in teaching and my creativity as a teacher, my past as a traveler, and my present friendships, relationships and community. Rediscovering my passions for Spanish and for the teaching profession this year has enriched my life.

I've always written, always wanted to be a writer. As a child, there were poems and stories, as a teen, there were diaries, as a traveler, there were journals. At one time, I liked writing letters. Sadly, my once steady correspondence has fallen by the wayside or morphed into email. As a student, I wrote papers and analyses. As a teacher, I taught writing, and learned a lot from that. Besides teaching, I've had a few jobs that have highlighted writing. I wrote for a theater company. I've done some freelance work. So I have written with a deadline. I still like writing freehand. But I love using a computer. For the past few years, much of my creative writing time has been devoted to products for our group.

Our writing/therapy group is perfect example of the way various strands in my life appear to be gathering into a single thread. For one thing, this group would never have happened if we weren't all at the same place at the same time at the elementary school where my children, my husband and I discovered community in Kansas, and where I now teach Spanish. In addition, through this group, I believe I've discovered both self-knowledge and creative strengths. The group has required discipline, and it has shown me that I can write regularly on demand, that I needn't always await the muse, that writing is both steady work and frequent joy. Our topics have helped me discover myself, to pinpoint the most significant incidents in my past and to see where they have taken me. I've been able to address some of my most painful as well as my most inspired memories and to share similar moments from the lives of other women. Writing these essays has helped me to realize who I am now, and why, and what I now believe. It has helped me to see what issues and which people are the most important to me in my life. And it has helped me to sense that I can accomplish writing goals. I have had ideas for books for years. But now, through personal growth over the past few years, I can imagine those books in print, and I believe I can get them written. The success of this group has inspired me.

You, my fellow authors, have inspired me.

BALANCE

Out of Kilter, Out of Steam

We can be sure that the greatest hope for maintaining equilibrium
in the face of any situation rests within ourselves.

—Frances J. Braceland

Patricia Antonopoulos

alance is a topic that won't stand up straight. It tilts. No matter how I try to make it otherwise, my sense of balance requires a disproportionate "give" from those who do not share my perspective.

Every four years we are assailed with the imbalance of November elections. Ever-new spins and deceptions hack away at our definition of patriotism. The intentions of that fledging 1776 government and the realities of today defy balance.

The great cathedrals are home to the 'high' side of worship while the storefront church neighbors with the food kitchen. Scripted prayers and choir hymns share the balance board with clapping hands and shouted Amens.

Ivy League schools may have some scholarship money, but the majority of students pay tuition from family pockets. Across town the dedicated educators struggle to find ways to keep the kids until graduation.

Global imbalance far outweighs any points of light we discover. People are hungry in a world where obesity is a health issue.

Perhaps the important thing about balance is that we continue the search, to believe in the possibility, hoping that personal harmony can translate into a kind of global equilibrium.

To seek balance is walking a walk, knowing that the destination moves ever forward with each step, always just out of reach.

Patti Dickinson

*B*alance is a list of sixty-one "Things to Do" sandwiched in between two soccer games, a track meet and a birthday party (and I don't have the gift bought or wrapped yet and we're out of tape, but I won't know that until I am done racing around in the car and back home). Balance cannot be achieved when that same "Things to Do" list goes through the washer and dryer, and I am on hands and knees, picking crispy white shreds of paper out of the lint catcher in an effort to bring some order to my day. Hoping that I'd written the list in permanent marker. Those are the days that I am not starting from a position of strength.

Balance is knowing that I have found the time to teach my adolescent children that mowing the lawn means mowing ALL the grass. Not just the grass they can get to without moving the basketball, the scooter, the hose, the gas can or their bike.

Balance is having quiet leadership and my wits about me at all times. Traveling in the car is one of those times. Chugging through the Plaza with five of my children in our blue Volvo station wagon, third row of seats facing backwards—saying, "Kathleen?" No answer. "Kathleeeeen?" Trying to keep the shrillness out of my voice and watch the road at the same time. Wondering how I'm going to make a U-turn in five o'clock traffic, because we must not HAVE Kathleen, or she'd be saying, "What?" "KATHLEEN." No question mark at the end. "Fooled you, Mommy!"

Balance is a meal with three things on the dinner plate. NOT shaped like a triangle and arriving in a cardboard box.

Balance is when both spouses sort of know how the day will play out. Who's driving who where, and at least once, exchanging a glance across the car or kitchen that both of you know translates into, "We wouldn't change a thing about this life of ours..." Maybe balance in a marriage means words are no longer as important as body language.

Balance is coming into the kitchen in the morning with no permission slips shoved under my nose as four different kids are trying to make lunches and be the first to get to the last of the Lucky Charms.

Balance is not missing one more seven-thirty a.m. orthodontist appointment.

Balance is teaching my children to put their things away, so that when we go to a hotel, they keep track of their belongings. Because then, their stuffed animal, specifically a bear named Oatmeal, won't get tangled up in sheets in an unmade bed, and the maid who comes in to change the sheets won't haul Oatmeal to Housekeeping in this ten thousand bed hotel on sheet-washing-day. No less than the general manager and his FOUR closest associates (all wearing suits) went to look for Oatmeal. Oatmeal was found. I think the fifty-dollar reward helped. Crisis averted.

Seeking balance is sort of second nature to the human condition. It allows us to experience the emotions of worry, anxiety, fear, potential loss and gratitude. Keeping us in touch with our humanity.

Shawna Samuel

This is a rich time in my life, which is mom-code for being very busy. Finding balance is a challenge. I have two children, volunteer at their schools in a variety of ways, am a den mother, etc. I am also on the altar guild at my church, an officer in my PEO chapter, attend a book club and have a part time job as city clerk of the city in which we live. I work from home, so I'm essentially a stay-at-home mom. In another time, raising children used to be enough. Now women feel compelled to have a list of accomplishments as long as their leg to justify their time at home. This current generation is geared to think of child rearing as a career. Several generations ago, children were expected to grow up as the adults saw to the business of living. Now, the expectations are high for what a stay-at-home mom should be doing.

All of my commitments might not sound like so much, and for the most part they aren't. But then there are those days when you have to have to build a Lincoln Memorial replica with the third graders at 10, have the cookies for their chat-and-chew at 11, pick-up, launder and return the linens for the church altar by noon, file books at the school library at 2 and give a report at a PEO meeting that night, following a brief attendance at book club. Oh yes, and let's not forget the ongoing demands of laundry, grocery shopping, cooking and cleaning. And, don't forget that we are supposed to get an hour of exercise a day, have a dog that needs walking, cats that need feeding, litter boxes that need cleaning, homework, scouting projects, selling popcorn and cookies. Oh and did I mention visiting a grandmother in a nursing home, working to have a good marriage, having some time for ourselves and each other, time for entertaining, and sharing with friends and family.

It makes me tired even thinking of all that we balance, from the miniscule details to serious childrearing worries. So why when our plates are so full do we still try to do so much? Our standards for ourselves are too high.

But before I climb aboard the martyr train, I have to admit that I get more out of life, feel more engaged and excited if I'm involved. I consider myself a work in progress, always learning, trying to improve. If I can learn from an experience, I will generally do it. I also need the balance that being involved in things that don't center around my family gives me. I need that for my own identity. And, honestly, it just feels plain good to give something back, to show some appreciation for all of the many blessings I have in my life.

My children are only this age once, and I know from experience that I will enjoy this trip so much more if I know their friends, spend time around them. I want that. I want that for me. And if I have to build a Lincoln Memorial or two, and bake 1,992 dozen cookies over my children's school years, so be it. It's worth it and it's a small price to pay. This isn't a dress rehearsal after all.

Jo Ann Stanley

*I*n the fall of 1995, I was shopping for groceries when a sudden wave of dizziness swept over me. I left the groceries and made it to the car. Two seconds later I was throwing up into a plastic bag that I happened to have in my vehicle. Convinced I had the flu, I tossed the bag into a convenient garbage can and drove home cautiously. Fortunately home was only a few minutes away.

That night I couldn't stop puking. Worse, when I tried to get to the bathroom, the whole room was spinning. I couldn't walk. I crawled into the bathroom and hugged the toilet. This was the most wicked flu I'd ever had.

My husband was out of town, and my kids still in elementary school. Fortunately it was my neighbor's turn to drive the carpool, so somehow I got the kids out of bed and on their way. There was a sink full of dirty dishes, the house was a mess, and I couldn't have cared less. I was still dizzy. I literally fell into bed. I couldn't keep anything down yet, but I assumed I'd sleep off the bug and eat later. Then I got the dry heaves.

That afternoon when the kids came home I was worse rather than better. I was weak, hadn't eaten anything, couldn't even sip water. The dizziness was incapacitating. As I tried to walk from my bedroom to the living room to greet them, I was banking from one side of the hallway to the other like a billiard ball on a pool table. My friend who had driven them home insisted on taking me right away to the doctor.

I had a hard time even in the waiting room. But when the doctor saw me he knew immediately what was wrong: an inner ear infection. (Either that or a brain tumor.) He said he could tell by the way my pupils were darting around the room, and had the nurse inject a motion sickness medication to get me stabilized. I got prescriptions for Antivert. He predicted that I'd be in bed for at least a week, and said I shouldn't drive for at least two. He thought my vertigo was probably caused by a viral infection that simply had to run its course.

There was one more long day until Kerry made it home. My neighbor took care of my kids at her house and she or her husband looked in on me frequently. I was the sickest I have ever been, before or since. It took me almost a month to get well, and at one point the doctor decided to go ahead and do tests for that brain tumor, including a CAT scan and another test where my head was hooked up to wires to measure my responses. I was terrified, but the tests were negative and eventually I felt better.

Within the inner ear lies the vestibular mechanism, a series of semicircular canals filled with fluid. By sensing head movements, this part of the human ear helps the body maintain its equilibrium. Motion and gravity are detected through the delicate mechanism. Thus when the inner ear becomes infected, the sense of balance is lost.

Now, whenever I am out of balance, I try listening to my inner ear. Another name for it might be "conscience." When life is out of whack, when I have questions about what I'm doing or how I'm handling a situation, I hear through my inner ear and somehow find my way.

FRIENDSHIP

A Gentle Refuge

My friends are my estate.

—Emily Dickinson

Patricia Antonopoulos

Friendship has always seemed a bit like a hand-me-down coat—serviceable, sometimes comfortable—but never exactly my own.

Our childhood neighborhood was rich with children, segregated male and female until twilight of long summer days. Games of hide and seek and kick the can filled the alley that divided the garages of Wilson Boulevard from those of 13th Street.

During those hot afternoons the boys huddled on the screened porch tacked to the Hughes home. Billy Jim and Butch hosted secret Club Meeting. Girls were not allowed.

The girls gathered under the shade of Lynn Peterson's giant elm tree to read and to wonder what that Club Meeting was about.

Maybe it was the heat, maybe boredom; maybe listening to Mert emote her favorite poem, The Highwayman, one more time.

Whatever the reason, we decided to demand to be in the Club. Negotiations began.

The boys devised a series of initiation tasks designed to scare us off but, if completed, could buy their friendship. Each time we successfully completed a task, another task would suddenly become part of the bargain. Several girls gave up and went back to our elm tree.

Mert and I stayed. At one point we took a break because my jump off Lynn's garage (alley side, not yard side) resulted in my bloody nose and chipped tooth. After a quick clean up in Mert's basement, we were back for what was promised to be the final challenge.

Climb up to the top bar of the swing set, get across that bar, one side to the other, and eat the surprise in the hollow of the pole. Mert went first, shimmied across and looked inside the opening, shook her head, climbed down and went home. Not one word.

My turn.

And so I ate that worm.

Know what they did at their Club Meetings? They read comic books! That's it—comic books. And I had to sit on the far side of the porch because I might be contaminated with worm juice.

High school and the first two years of college were good times for discovering friendships. Then I married and the next years were filled with friendships of circumstance-walking babies, church things, school activities. There were no lasting couples friends. Circumstances.

Back to college when my children were in school, but that was a different experience. Taking classes while the kids were in school, studying while they slept. Friendship did not fit well.

Teaching was a time of great joy and I loved those classroom hours. Many wonderful and dedicated educators shared those circumstance friendships.

Retirement was a time to care for my mother and to offer "friendship" to the residents of the nursing home. Perhaps it was reciprocal, but it often felt one sided. These were people with huge needs and I was a source.

And then circumstance began the redefinition of friendship in the person of Patti Dickinson.

Suddenly, I could share secrets both sad and glorious. I could offer my successes and my shames without rejection. She confidently shared as much with me.

I laughed at her nonsense and cried with her insight. Patti validated me in a way that no other person had done. Together we learned that the destination is too far if the beginning point is not embraced. I found the word, "heartspeak" by journeying with integrity.

Together we walked into a new place—a place that revived through rearrangement, grew though attrition—an oasis named Cedar Row.

I found Shawna who is periwinkle, the color of confidence—beautiful, open and straight forward, fiercely loyal—who has walked that search for self knowledge. . .who can restate the feelings of others with words of support and understanding. Shawna has taken the power to be the woman that she has chosen.

I found Jo Ann—the adventurer, the traveler, the dedicated friend—a woman who treasures family and friends, who loves the richness of language and has a flair for fun in the dramatic, who can be straightforward and outspoken, who can melt into tears when sharing someone's pain, who found a guitar-strumming soul mate.

My new coat has the feel of silk and the look of tailor made.

Patti Dickinson

Friendship is crucial to a woman's well being. Friendship is emotional intimacy that needs nurturing and gentleness. I have that sort of friendship. It sustains me. It validates. She is a companion who reflects so many of my beliefs. She is strong when I am not. She redirects me when something in my life is making me too harsh a judge, or too condemning of myself. She has held my hand with both of hers. She has said the exact-right-perfect words. She has shielded me from life's abrasiveness. Human sandpaper, she is. When all I see is the one thing that I've screwed up, she points out the ten good things I've managed to accomplish. There is a rhythm and a cadence to a friendship such as this. This isn't a friendship of convenience—we don't carpool our kids, or co-lead a Brownie troop. Nor is it a couples' friendship. This is she and I.

I can remember a high school friendship that allowed me to share the angst I felt over the train wreck that was my parents' marriage. She had the same situation—palpable hostility. We breathed the same emotional air. She knew—without hearing every detail. She understood. "Me too" was a refrain spoken often between us. We were sophomores in high school. We talked of boyfriends and how far was too far. Certainly not information we were getting at home. Home was a battleground, not a place to ask questions. Blades of grass served as male/female stand-ins. We sat in her driveway on a summer evening, discussing sexual morality with blades of grass—boy on top, girl on top—with CLOTHES, of course. In Catholic vernacular, we were trying to find that line in the sand that signified the dreaded "near occasion of sin." We smoked our first cigarette together, unfiltered Tareyton's in a field at 103rd and Roe. We tried out for Sion Singers together. Neither one of us could carry a tune; we just liked the dresses. Pale pink shirtwaist affairs with a skirt that would billow out if you spun around. I was first. I began singing, "Oh, say can you see. . ." and could see her, across the room, back turned, her hands covering her mouth, presumably to muffle the HYSTERICS she was in, her whole body shaking. Then that unmistakable gasp for air, followed by more shaking. End of audition, because I couldn't get another word out, and couldn't compose myself. The choir director was NOT amused.

She gave birth to a daughter two weeks before we adopted our first. We spent three days a week together —traveling in my blue Volvo station wagon, because it would easily transport two strollers. We were companions; we talked of baby stages and phases. We were on the same housecleaning schedule. Vacuuming on Mondays. Kid naps from one to three. We talked every day on the phone. We still see each other three times a year. Always dinner at a Mexican restaurant. We've shared much over baskets of chips and salsa. That friendship has lasted thirty-five years. No longer a day-to-day friendship—it now is sustained only by memories. A shared history. We went from first bras to first babies in what now seems like the blink of an eye.

Once my kids started school, my social life seemed to focus around conversations on the sidewalk of the elementary school, soccer field and basketball court. Committees, ranging from chairing pancake breakfasts to teaching CCD. I had hit my stride, and was well on my way to a Ph.D. in volunteerism. Some wonderful company, some beautiful, poignant moments of sharing, but most of those friendships required accomplishing something at school to gather us together.

In many ways, I have been out of sync. By the time we had our eighth baby, most of the friends that I had early on had gone back to work. They were driving with teenagers, I was still trying to get a screaming two year old strapped into a car seat. Yet I didn't want to talk diapers and teething and preschools with those who had kids my youngest's age. Been there, done that. By the time Margaret came along, my oldest was fourteen. I didn't need friendship for the same reasons. I no longer cared who had a three week old that could read, or a newborn that could tie her shoes. I wanted companionship, someone that could talk about something other than the kid-related stuff.

In much the same way high school kids seek friendship from those who have similar interests, that's the direction friendship took for me, as well. No longer interested in peers just because we had kids the same age, or on the same soccer team, I screened potential friends differently now. Maybe that was because I had so little discretionary time that I wanted to be sure that I was spending that time with people that filled that social, intellectual, emotional need. All of this in retrospect—I have no remembrance of consciously making that decision—it just sort of evolved. Alliances were formed because there was a shared interest—such as knitting or running or a connection that was mutually recognized.

Not surprisingly, my closest friends all have big families. Maybe because I am often uncomfortable with the world's perception of who I am. I fidget when someone says, "I just don't know how you do it. . ." I hit the ground running seven days a week. It feels like what I was destined to do. I chose this and don't want any applause for that choice. Washing a hundred and twelve socks a week isn't heroic. (Although solving the issue of why only one hundred and nine of them actually exited the dryer just might be lower-level heroism.) I run in, breathless, to just about everything any of my kids do of an extracurricular nature, and I hope that my kids don't remember that part, only that I am there, winded, but present.

I believe that those "me, too" friendships are miraculous. Someone with whom I can be silent. Where words are not necessary. My friends understand, maybe intrinsically, that because I am a blurter, I will share what I am withholding —all when the time is right. So there is an unspoken understanding—don't ask. I will tell. I have shared friendships with women who knew just exactly when the right time was to call, just what to say, and when to say nothing. When I needed the resounding echo of silence because there were no words—my friend, my soul mate knew to say nothing. Sometimes sharing silence, and the implied understanding— the need for no words, is the most precious gift of all.

Shawna Samuel

*W*hen I was growing up, I was the sort of kid who never had a group to run with, but always had a best friend or two, girls who meant the whole world to me. One is still a kindred spirit, Judy. In third grade, she was the girl with the rainbow pastel notebook paper who I thought was totally neat. Now, thirty-five years later, she's a woman I can share anything with, who speaks to my heart, and I to hers. We have been through a lot together, and shared some sorrows like infertility. And some sorrows we have only shared through close letters and talks, trying to support one another. She's the sort of person who will go shopping with you to help you pick out new eyeliner, and then when you get home, she'll give you all of her good brushes so you can try it out right away.

Being the sensitive kid that I was, I was open for much heartache when it came to friendships during school. When I went away to college, I made a resolution that I was not going to try to change myself to fit in. I was going to be totally myself, for better or for worse. And for the first time ever, I had a real group of friends to run with. And they've turned out to be friends for life. Mary Beth, Chris, Susie, women who seemed to like me, quirks and all. I felt accepted like I never had before. I am still extremely close to those special women. We live in different cities today, and see each other only a couple of times a year, but when we do, it's as if we've never been apart. They fill me up more than a year's worth of therapy ever could. I need those women in my life, crave them, and always have them in my thoughts and near my heart, every day. There's nothing I couldn't share with them. We have something so special and so strong, that I cherish them, and feel blessed by them.

When I finished college, married Duncan and was working, I had a difficult dry spell, lacking of the joy of women friends. I was just getting to know my neighbors, many of whom already had children. I had friendships at work, but the office politics complicated those. Duncan's friends were older, many with teenagers, so that was awkward. When I had Caitlin, a short two years later, I was totally lost. No other woman I knew was having a baby. I retired, so any work associates were history. I was lonely beyond description. I went through that desperate time looking for another mom who might share some interests, and nap schedules. It was worse than dating. It was worse than blind dating! It wasn't until Caitlin started school that my friendships with women really started to take off. It was so much more natural and easy.

As you age and mellow, so do friendships. It becomes more about acceptance for who you are rather than defining who you should be. It stops being competitive and starts being comforting. Really true, good friends accept all sides of you.

This became most apparent to me on an awful day when I'd become involved in a controversial situation with the Homes Association that had escalated into a terrible, emotional mess. I'd dealt with it all day, putting on a good face, saying all the right things. My college friend, Chris, called from Chicago to talk about an upcoming trip we had planned. She thought I should fly into a different airport, change airlines. I just lost it. All the emotions I'd held in check all day spilled out, and I yelled, accusing her of changing her mind after I'd already purchased tickets, and on and on I went. What I was met with was not anger, or judgment, but understanding. It was an immediate response of, "Okay, what's up? What's wrong? Talk to me. Let's work this out together." That was when I knew what grown-up friendship was.

I've lived in my home 18 years. I've seen neighbors come and go. You can talk over getting the newspaper or mowing the lawn, but the word neighbor was redefined one day when Duncan had an accident. It was during a January ice storm. Over a Thursday, odd temperature conditions had caused more than two inches of ice to form over everything. The kids had been home from school that day, due to the weather. Much to my relief, Duncan came home around 5:00. He changed clothes, put on clean sweats that I'd washed that day, and thought he'd go and fill the car with gas. I thought he should stay home. I had started dinner, and all my "chicks" were in their nest, and I liked it that way. But he walked out the front door, and I went in the kitchen to start dinner. It was then that I heard a huge, explosive pop, then leaves rustling, sticks breaking, then a chest-rattling thud. I ran to the door. My eyes were filled with branches. The car was covered in them. It's funny, but I felt sure Duncan was fine. I yelled out, in sort of a dramatic, isn't this amazing sort of way, "Are you OK?" "I don't think so." This is when everything felt like it was moving in slow motion. I couldn't see him, but it sounded like he was on the ground around the car.

Getting around the car was difficult. My obvious path was blocked with all the branches from the huge tree limb that had fallen. I squeezed around the other way, and first saw his head, resting on his arms, face down. As I got closer, and saw more of his body, he looked OK. Then I saw his leg. His calf was pinned under the jagged end of the branch, the largest part that had been ripped away from the trunk of the tree due to the heavy coating of ice. It was as big around as a turkey platter. His calf looked like it was about two inches thick, and his foot was facing backwards. He was awake and calm. He'd hit his forehead and was bleeding, and his hands were bloody. For an instant, I looked around, and in the quiet of the storm, ice muffling every sound, I felt absolutely alone. I thought about yelling for help, but not only felt no sound could come from my throat, but I was afraid I'd scare Duncan.

I tried lifting the branch. Couldn't. I looked around. Nobody. I looked at his leg. I had to lift the branch. So I grabbed it from underneath and did the deep knee bend of my life. That branch moved up like it was a feather. I was holding it, and asked him to scoot out. He said he couldn't. Then he looked behind him, saw me holding this thing, and managed to crawl forward a bit, just enough to clear the branch as I gently put it down. His leg followed him like a disconnected rag.

Then I wasn't alone any more. Friends were there. Laura, our next-door-neighbor had her window open and phone in her hand. "Do you want me to call someone?" "Yes" I said, noting that she didn't say 911—keep Duncan calm. She was relaying questions from the paramedics: Is he conscious? How old is he? She'd already called Tom Woolwine, the only other man she knew was home at the time. I looked up and here he came, sort of running, but everything was so slick with ice that it looked more like an exaggerated, high gallop. "We're here Shawna, you aren't alone. You aren't alone. We're here. . .What can I do? What do you need?" I asked him to go in and get a big comforter to cover Duncan, and then get my purse. I was incredibly clear thinking and calm. Duncan told me to get out from under the tree. I told him I wasn't leaving him, no matter what. Tom Stewart from across the street was there, thinking about getting some plywood to cover us if more branches fell. Duncan asked me if his leg was bleeding. "It doesn't look like it," I said. I could hear the sirens at that point, an amazingly comforting sound in that situation. A stranger driving by stopped, came over and asked if he could help. Who was he?

The fire truck and ambulance pulled up. Thank God. They assessed Duncan, who seemingly wasn't in much pain, and wanted to be moved before he was stabilized because he was afraid more of the tree was going to fall on him. They asked me to get away, so I went in and talked to the children. I told them that

Dad had broken his leg and was going to the hospital. Laura would be over to get them, and they would stay with her. I'd be back later, and everything was going to be fine. They seemed okay, not scared or upset. By that time, Duncan was on a stretcher, and Tom Bender came down to give me a hug. "Duncan broke his leg" was all I could say. I sat in the front seat of the ambulance for a long time, while they stabilized his leg in a funky looking foam cast. The cast went to a 90-degree angle to the right, an angle no normal leg could ever accomplish. Duncan was shaking, and I was afraid that he'd go into shock. They assured me he was fine.

We drove slowly to St. Luke's. I remember holding Duncan's hand as they wheeled him into the hospital. That was the first time we both felt scared.

It was a bad break. His tibia and fibula were each broken in three places, and all three had punctured the skin. The break by his ankle was the worst, as the bone had been crushed. Duncan was in the operating room within the hour, and the surgeon told us that a break this bad would require a titanium rod through the middle of the bone, with screws at both ends to hold it. The biggest risk was infection, since the bones had come through the skin. There couldn't be a cast, due to the open wounds, and Duncan would be lucky if the bones ever healed because there is poor blood flow in the lower leg. But he warned us; infection was the biggest threat, and the first of many hurdles.

Late that night, Tom Miller came out in the storm to take me home. Our children had stayed with them. Laura told me that they'd been watching from an upstairs window when they turned Duncan over. The blood on his face had scared them, and they were upset. I can't think of anyone else I would rather have comfort them than Laura. I took the kids home and began a long night of worry and fear, as more branches fell on our house that night.

The next day, Alex came down with a terrible flu with a high fever. Caitlin followed shortly thereafter, and we had no electricity. But my friends and neighbors were at my side in so many ways, it's hard to enumerate them. Some cleaned up my yard and all the debris. Two grown men together couldn't lift the branch that I'd lifted alone the night before. I couldn't lift it the next day either. Jo Ann and Sue watched my sick children while I went to the hospital. They brought food, care packages. Jane, a former nurse, looked at Duncan's wounds one day when I was worried. Then she stayed and did my dishes and cleaned up my kitchen, and listened while I lay on the sofa and talked. Patti walked my dog every day. Laura gave me her cell phone for the week, since my phone line was out. Bob, a doctor, came over when Duncan was coming home from the hospital to help me get him upstairs to our room. He'd been in the hospital ten days, and was very weak. Bob's wife, Suzanne, ran errands for me, and wouldn't let me pay her. Merrill also shopped and cooked for me, and so did her mom. Jennifer did therapeutic touch as Duncan was healing. Sue and Gary drove across town one night to be sure we had dinner. They literally held me up, for weeks and months.

I look back on that time with mixed feelings. Duncan has since made a full recovery, but it was a year-long process. He never fought the infection we so desperately feared, possibly because the sweatpants he was wearing had been freshly laundered. It was the most traumatic time of my life, but the heartwarming feelings I have for all of my friends easily overcome all of that. I can stand at a party with Tom Woolwine, and still see him galloping over the ice yelling, "You're not alone. . . .." and I just want to hug him. I feel differently about my community, my neighborhood, the world. These peoples' lives were a mess also. They didn't have electricity, food to eat or cook, or clean clothes to wear. But they were there for me.

And this writing group. We have transformed from pleasant acquaintances saying hi in the school parking lot to soul mates by sharing our stories. It's been an honor to be the recipient of their inner thoughts. It's been humbling and therapeutic to share mine. And it's been life changing to experience the complete trust and acceptance of whatever has been said. Each has brought her own unique gift to the group. Like flowers in a bouquet, we all began as closed-tight buds just beginning to open. Pat, a red rose, a passionate, complicated combination of sturdy backbone, with some thorns from past hurts and fragile, sensitive, beautiful petals. Patti, a bright pink peony, large, complex and full of life. The symbol of energy and good will. Who has a huge capacity for love and a never-ending spirit to get it right. Who brings new meaning to multi-tasking. And Jo Ann, the clematis. The traveler, who weaves a tendril of adventure into everything she does. Who has a passion and zest for friends, life, learning and words that is inspirational. Who blooms bright purple with the love of her wonderful husband, and her two girls.

It is through the warmth of our sharing, of allowing ourselves to be vulnerable, trusting in one another, and accepting and supporting one another that our bouquet has opened into a full and glorious bloom.

Jo Ann Stanley

Friendship dwells in this cozy shop with its riot of colors, textures, and patterns. For friendship, I'm minding the store while the owner travels to Guatemala. In friendship, I will pass the key to another who will mind shop next Saturday. We're the warp, woof and weft on this loom of interconnected friendship.

Friendship flirts when you meet someone new, and you hit it off. There's a connection there that is immediate, but only time can tell whether you have made an acquaintance or a friend. Friendship endures. Time and distance are threats to friendship that may be overcome. With long-standing friends, you can recover the time apart; pick up where you left off. Call it "The Big Chill" factor.

Friendship falters in the painful moment when I have to tell my friend that her cat is dead. I'm twenty-two and caring for Stargazer for a few days while my girlfriend is out of town. Friday, after a long day of classes and work, I come home tired and let Stargazer out the back door of the farmhouse, not realizing that another housemate has a friend over whose big black Labrador is roaming the property.

Delicate Stargazer was no match for Brandy! The dog's most basic hunting instincts must have taken over in the tall grasses of the farm. When I found the cat's broken body, I couldn't understand at first what had happened. To this day this incident is one of my most guilt-ridden memories. But friendship forgives, and my friend and I remain close. Together, we buried Stargazer.

Friendship rescues. It's Nancy's voice on the other end of the line saying yes when you need a favor, big or small. It's Sheila or Joan, someone you could call in an emergency. It's bringing dinner to a new mom in the neighborhood. It's helping Merrill move. On Wednesdays, it's babysitting for Eliot, whose big blue eyes laugh at me. He'll be one year old on Monday.

With Eliot's mom, friendship has been bumpy. She's a single mom, loaded with stress and strain. She's having difficulty finding work and has limited financial resources. She and her husband began having difficulties during the pregnancy, and they separated just after the baby was born. The divorce is pending. They are embroiled in an acrimonious legal battle over their most important asset, their son. I see it as such a sad, even tragic situation, and my heart goes out to all, but especially to Eliot. My husband and I have tried to remain impartial with the parents, maintaining friendships with both mom and dad. This autumn I was babysitting every Wednesday, each time bringing lunch or a gift, trying to be a caring, supportive friend to my girlfriend in need. So it hurt when we sat on the couch a few days before Christmas and she told me she could no longer be my friend because I was still friendly with her ex. Both of us were brought to tears. It's been a long time since I've felt that kind of hurt.

Since then we've resumed our friendship. I think she realized that I wasn't taking sides, and I believe that she missed me. She has called and we've gotten together a few times and I've started watching the baby occasionally. Something in our friendship might have been lost, but we are trying to find it again.

Friendship shares; there's give and take. With my women friends, I'm always growing. We discuss, we dissect, we complain, we listen, we advise and we learn from each other. It's book club once a month on Tuesday, and my political discussion group on Wednesday. And it's Thursday words and Thursday tears when this circle of friends comes together to read our stories. It's support, it's laughter, it's therapy, it's a form of love. Friendship is the buoy that keeps us all afloat.

SOLITUDE

Finding Self

There are days when solitude is a heady wine that intoxicates you with freedom,
others when it is a bitter tonic,
and still others when it is a poison that makes you beat your head against the wall.

—**Colette,** *Earthly Paradise, 1966*

Patricia Antonopoulos

Solitude is fluid, sometimes even tidal in the rhythm and flow, and all about expectation. The frame of solitude has little to do with shared or empty space. The shift from being alone to being lonely is but a shift in expectation.

When my life has emotional and spiritual richness, I can list tens of ideas for renewal, for moving from loneliness. Yet these are the times when I have little need for renewal, when loneliness is close to an abstraction. These are the times I have honored my spiritual and emotional self.

When solitude is comfort, I relish and am renewed by my time wrapped in the quiet cold of the ice rink, my hours at the River Walk, the comfort of rereading a favorite book.

If empty days congeal a shell of isolation, no matter the people and demands of my time, I probably cannot be renewed. There simply is no act of renewal. There is only getting through it, clinging to deeply held values and persisting—a time for the 15-minute Rule of Life: Anything is possible for 15 minutes; just persevere.

These are the times of needing to be lost in physical work—cleaning my space to hide from my heart. Intense exercise is my other escape, a form of running to keep myself at bay.

A holiday, any holiday, can tick off the seconds dragging towards tomorrow if I am emotionally alone, feeling abandoned by circumstance. Holidays carry such an unfair burden of expectation.

Peanut butter piled on a wheat bagel and a cup of hot lemon water are the perfect lunch when I choose to eat alone. I can be choked, unable to swallow the best of meals if my beloved and I are silent at the table, not trusting enough to share a feeling.

Ironically, this emptiness is the welcome mat for soul-growth, the opening to new understanding and acceptance. Forgiveness is probably the hidden passage from loneliness, a process that heals the silence. But it is so dark in that passageway.

Forgiveness of self is most neglected. By early training, many of us have learned to hide hurt and anger, insuring that a huge portion of self is left untended, unrecognized. Intimacy dies in that place of neglect, and loneliness fills the void.

At this moment, I believe that the stages of love and trust influence the comfort of, and the need for, being alone. When intimacy and trust are richly honored, being alone can be welcomed. If either intimacy or trust has been betrayed, loneliness is as dark as any heartache.

Patti Dickinson

Solitude: n. but plays out as a v. Used to:

Regroup,
sift through cognitive clutter,
debrief,
savor the quiet,
wear the finish off the floor pacing,
chew my cuticles,
detangle the strings of a complicated life,
make a definitive to-do list,
glue my emotional self back together,
beat myself up,
walk—fast and with purpose,
examine my motives,
wonder at life's blessings,
mourn what wasn't that should have been,
sit on the porch and watch the world,
zigzag around doing two hours of cleaning/picking up in ten minutes,
whirlwind through the grocery store,
take inventory,
celebrate a lightbulb moment,
wander the aisles of a bookstore,
wonder at the tenacity of a squirrel trying to get at the bird feeder
enjoy the tactile pleasures of a knitting shop,
send an e-mail communiqué of substance,
warm my hands on a steaming mug of coffee on a chilly winter morning
mow the lawn, grass clippings clinging to my shins
dig in the dirt,
probe the shadows,
be,
take a nap,
second guess
connect the dots.

Shawna Samuel

I crave alone time, need alone time, but I am extremely afraid of being alone, of living alone.

I probably crave alone time because I hardly ever have it. And I'm thankful for that. I live with my husband, two children, two cats, a dog and a couple dozen fish. I have never lived alone in my entire life. I went from my mother's home, to a college roommate, to being married. I don't think I'd like it. At all.

Granted, some of my most productive times are when I'm alone. I have learned that I have to be alone to really think things through, to write, to work. I like my own company, love being in my own home, enjoy the simple pleasures of housework when I'm not pushed and stressed. I hardly ever go to a party alone, never to a movie or restaurant alone, and I don't really want to. I am thankful every day that I don't live alone. I love having family around me—the more, the better. I would have had more children if it had worked out. I shudder to think of what it will be like to have my kids out in the world somewhere doing their own things, and not safely tucked in each night. I want time to freeze.

Frankly, I get a little weird when I'm alone too much of the time. I need to talk to and be with others. If I go a day or two without much of that, I begin to avoid it, and I can get into a bad cycle.

One of the things I like most about being married is the companionship; and I happen to have a very companionable husband. I almost didn't marry him because he was older by 16 years and I didn't want to think about being alone when I'm old. But I realized that you don't base important decisions on odds and probabilities 50 years down the road. Who knows, I could be run over by a bus tomorrow. He could be the one left behind.

Although I don't entertain these thoughts often, sometimes it scares me thinking about being alone. How sad it is to think of older people who have children who don't come around much. People who have buried most of their friends and a good deal of their family. Will that be me? I pray not.

At Thanksgiving last year, someone started the deal where during grace we each had to go around the table and say one thing we were thankful for. Immediately what came to my mind was the fact that I have a family to be with, that I don't live alone in the world. It struck me as strange that I would think that, as it is not a conscious thought or worry. But there it was, clear as day.

As I write this, it is a cool, early fall type of day. The fall always brings that old nostalgic back-to-school, in-for-the-night type of feeling. Plus, a lot of my friends' children have been leaving for their first year of college. It's brought me to tears, and I'm still a few years away from that. Only three though, and counting. And the quiet of the house feels weird as the noise of a busy summer still hangs in the air. Last night I fixed a nice dinner, we all stayed in, enjoyed each other. What will I do when I don't have a family to cook for? What will it be like when that in-for-the-night feeling is coupled with the feeling of what it's like to be alone? Truly alone. Maybe I'll never know. Maybe.

Jo Ann Stanley

5:40 a.m. Raucous music disturbs my slumber. Dagnabbit. My teen has switched my radio station again, and the noise is obnoxious. I slam the sleep switch and doze through the next six minutes, anticipating the alarm this time and turning it off before it can disturb me again. Comatose hubby manages to sleep through the radio. And the grumbling.

I'm up. I do that foot stretch thing that helps with chronic heel pain. I hear my fourteen-year-old daughter in the shower as I open the door to my older daughter's room. My sixteen- year-old has ignored her alarm again, but she hears me come in and flips over, ready for her favorite way to wake up—massage therapy. I acquiesce and give her mom's special five- minute shoulder rub.

I need coffee, stumble downstairs, while she goes into the other shower. As the coffee drips, I feed the dog and the cat, maybe unload the dishwasher. Then I allow myself time to sip one slow cup of java magic while sitting on the living room couch, usually reading or studying, sometimes joined by one of my daughters for a few moments of morning companionship. I then do everything I can to help them get ready, from cooking breakfast to finding clean outfits or underwear, to braiding hair, to making lunch, upstairs, downstairs, down the basement, while the girls get dressed, primp, and organize their five-million pound backpacks. Some days my husband wakes up just in time to say goodbye. Other days he's gone before we are, or else he's off on a business trip and there's less competition for the bathroom. Now the girls and I take off in the station wagon, scarier than you think with a teen practicing her driving. I leave them at school, then return, but I can't relax yet: I am greeted by the dog with her tongue hanging out. I grab the leash and a baggie for our round trip to the park.

Then, finally…

SOLITUDE. Solitude in one of its purest, headiest forms: the back-to-school variety. Knowing where your children are, for over six hours. Hoping they are profitably employed, but more important, fully certain they are supervised. Having time to clean, sort the mail, attack the closets, but instead sitting outside on the screened porch with a second cup of coffee and a good book. Wandering into the kitchen and seeing an empty sink rather than one overflowing with dishes. Appreciating how nice the refrigerator looks with its door shut. Listening to your own music on the CD player, or none at all. Enjoying full access to your computer, keeping up with your email or surfing the net at will. Watching Perry Mason reruns while you're ironing, or simply allowing the TV to hibernate. Knowing that when and if the telephone rings, it's for you, even if it's only a telemarketer, and recognizing with joy that an entire day might go by when it does not ring at all. Feeling sassy and secure in the knowledge that you could eat a full quart of Haagen-Dazs Rum Raisin all by yourself and buy a replacement before anyone ever noticed. Knowing that if you want to take the car out of the driveway, it's for your own errand, not because you are someone else's chauffeur. Best of all, there is time to think. Time that's precious to me. I can direct my own activities, determine priorities, and keep home and family happy without any interference from actual family members. On my good days, I begin with exercise. Some days I actually make it to the gym.

Most days I love walking solo, perhaps allowing my thoughts to drift, but more often channeling my thinking and incubating ideas. The rhythm stimulates my creativity; often my best teaching and writing tricks flow from this process. When I get home all I have to do is type whatever it is into the computer. I like to be alone when I'm working on the computer. When my family is around I don't think as well; there are too many distractions and often someone else with a computer priority.

I would not want to live alone, or even be alone for long, but I enjoy my school day solitude. When I feel stressed or depressed, I like to be alone with my thoughts. When I need to clear my head, there is nothing better than a long walk.

My image of the most calming kind of solitude is me, by myself, out of breath from the hike, sitting on a rock in a mountain meadow. There's a light breeze and maybe the hum of an insect. Purple lupine mixes with cow parsnip in the field where marmots frolic, and the snow capped peaks surround me in their majestic silence. My thoughts slow until they are still; I'm practically meditating. I feel only awe, and I become very small in relation to what is around me.

MARRIAGE

The Truth About
"For Better Or For Worse"

Of all serious things,
Marriage is the funniest.

—Beaumarchais, *The Marriage of Figaro*

Patricia Antonopoulos

For better or for worse. . .
till death do us part. . .

A promise, a vow made with no caveat, no escape clause, and no excuse.

Both of my grandmothers lived sad and seemingly empty lives, moving parallel with husbands who did not display affection or share joy. One grandmother rarely spoke and took comfort from food. The other grandmother became a bitter vindictive woman who seemed to poison the lives around here. Both grandmothers stayed in their marriage. They kept their vows.

Even as a young child, I felt sad for my grandmothers. In my childish way, I attempted to comfort them, having some understanding of their sadness. Despite knowing that my grandfathers did not treat their wives with any affection, I relished the time with my grandfathers. I loved them dearly.

My mother stayed with my dad, though they had some problems in their marriage. They truly loved one another, but alcohol did create the sharpest edges in their lives.

In 1958, I made the marriage promise for the first time. I was 19 and he was 26, a navy veteran. Twenty-three years later, I broke the promise, deciding that ". . . for worse" did not mean *this* bad.

There are those who would say that situations and behaviors can break the covenant of marriage. That could be my excuse, but I do not remember the priest mentioning any deal breakers. Things happened in my marriage that were definitely covered in the ". . .for worse" part of the promise and I make a decision to break the vow.

A guarded place in my heat wishes that I had honored the vow and let death be the deal breaker. The regret mis real. What if I had tried one more time? What if . . . ? But I did not.

My reasons for divorce now seem like throw-away details compared to the marred lives of my children. Ripples from that divorce continue to feel like whirlpools threatening to drown us in some unspoken part of the past.

Divorce ended a marriage and irrevocably marked the lives of the innocents. The pain of this breach must not have been enough.

Making the promise for a second time was done with no less sincerity that the first time. Maybe I accepted that ". . . for better of for worse. . . " might be a bitter bargain, but I wanted to love again.

Divorce took away the intact family—the security of the known.

Remarriage took away the new security we has been building together. Now there was another person restructuring my children's lives, eroding the tentative new safe place.

My children care deeply, even love my husband. They refer to us as *Our Parents* or *Our Folks*. We have been rebuilding again, but the foundation cannot be changed. And that foundation holds much of their lives . . . for better or for worse.

Patti Dickinson

He saves everything,
I throw it away if it isn't going to be used in the next hour and a half.

I am neat, way neat

And he is not, way not.

I pinch pennies and he doesn't.

He uses the parking brake, I don't.

I am a morning person and he isn't.

I am out of bed talking; he needs two cups of coffee and an hour before he's coherent.

I read mostly non-fiction and memoirs. He reads science fiction and historical stuff.

He can tell which direction is north. I do the left-right method of getting places.

I mow recklessly, creating geometric patterns all over the yard on a whim.

He mows from the perimeter in: never varies, won't even change directions.

I dig up dandelions; he sprays them.

I have a calendar. A paper one. He has a calendar, an electronic one.

I have a cell phone that rarely leaves the house or the charger. He has a pager, and a
    cell phone. Constantly ringing, playing tunes, beeping, vibrating.

He opens every single piece of mail that slides into the mail slot, even the stuff
    that comes to Occupant. I stand over the trash sorting mail.

He listens to every single song on a CD.

I listen to the one, maybe two songs I like over and over.

He checks the Internet for the weather; I look out the window.

I like to talk; he likes to listen.

He reads six books at a time. I read one. I never, ever break that rule.

He makes three trips to the hardware store for every home repair; I have unplugged
    the stopped-up kitchen garbage disposal with a toilet bowl plunger—TWICE.

I can't remember what any movie I've ever seen was about.

He remembers every movie he's ever seen. Going back YEARS.

He doesn't like spaghetti. How could I have married a man that doesn't like spaghetti?

He always shovels the snow off the driveway, the back step, and the front sidewalk.

I let the sun melt it.

I like strawberry jam. He likes grape jelly.

He puts peanut butter and jelly on different sides of the bread.

I put them on the same side.

He never drives more than FOUR miles over the speed limit. I plead the Fifth.

He is rarely ever in the last quarter of the tank of gas.

I drive on fumes. (And I've NEVER run out of gas.)

I can beat him at backgammon blindfolded. He can beat me at Crazy Eights.

I tell him one is a game of skill, the other a game of chance. Guess which is which.

He hurries never. I hurry always.

He under-packs. I over-pack.

I use the phone book. He uses directory assistance.

I can't read with ANY noise—not music, not conversation.

He reads with chaos surrounding him.

I can't sleep in a car or on a plane. He can.

I use windshield wipers at the first sprinkle. He uses them on intermittent, in a deluge.

I read the newspaper from cover to cover. He skims the headlines and gets

    his news from the radio.

He uses a travel agent; I arrange it myself.

I balance the checkbook, he doesn't.

He is a night owl. I haven't seen in the new year in a decade.

I make the bed every morning. He sees it as a completely unnecessary chore.

I unravel; he gets quiet.

I laugh out loud; he chuckles.

I am a backseat driver; he is not.

I blurt it out; he chooses his words carefully.

I am a first-born; he is a last-born.

I like the house at a temperature that he considers cold enough to hang meat.

He wears a sweatshirt.

He loves to eat a big breakfast. I am a purist. Coffee only, until noon.

I am impulsive—he is methodical.

He likes Halloween. I like Christmas.

He likes fall. I like spring.

We bought our house with our hearts.

We both think that this is a forever kind of house.

We both believe in happy endings. Well, most of the time.

We both love vanilla ice cream with black specks.

We both knew that eight was enough.

We both know the importance of every day.

We both prefer a distressed antique to a polished Ethan Allen.

We both can eat candy corn until our fillings scream.

We both love our children so much it sometimes hurts.

We both thought we believed in using cloth diapers. We both changed our minds
within two diaper changes of that first kid.

We both think cottage cheese is repulsive. Neither of us has tasted it.

We both love the color blue.

We both love Chatham, Massachusetts, the ocean and salty air blowing on our faces.

We both love to collect driftwood and the feel of sand between our toes.

We both love black and white photographs.

We both love thunderstorms.

There have been times when our differences felt like they could be our undoing.

And times when our sameness has felt like all there was to cling to.

Shawna Samuel

Marriage is a mixed bag. It's different than I thought it would be in some ways, and just like I thought it would be in others. I feel blessed to have fallen for such a good man, for my husband is, before all else, truly good. He is kind-hearted, faithful, and a devoted, loving father. We have the normal amount of frustrations, I suppose. He's married to a type A person, has a type A job, and is not a type A man. You've got to give him credit for just hanging in with life. Being the type B or even C man, he can be a bit overwhelmed with the logistics of life. He doesn't multi-task well (and this means using the car remote to unlock the car doors while walking. It's a full stop, point, push then walk) so the daily basics can overwhelm him. But when he's happy, relaxed, and surrounded by his family, all is right with his world. This is when he truly shines, and the core aspect of his being shows through.

We've been through some sad times together, like family deaths, infertility, loss of jobs, an accident, but we always turn towards each other rather than away. A sadness in our marriage is that he's 16 years older than I am. We tried to fight that for four years in the beginning of our relationship, both thinking that it was too great a span to be together for life. But our love just kept pulling us toward each other until we finally gave in. However, the age difference gives us different needs, different circles, and these can widen as you get older.

Most importantly, we are the best of friends. We like the same things, enjoy being together, talking, we both have a sense of humor. We definitely laugh more than anything else we do. He's a great companion, and I think he'd say the same of me. After all, it's not every couple who can watch Miss America one night, and Monday night football the next, both enjoying and sharing in all the dramas.

We never really fight. We have disagreements over silly things, like how to hang pictures, but all of our disagreements are so tame we can easily have them in front of the children. It is probably good for them to see two people working out conflict in a respectful way. My husband's parents never fought, so he's still learning that conflict can be positive. After our first argument, he was convinced that we were not meant for each other.

With our many shared likes, we do have a lot of differences. He talks in a deliberate, thoughtful, slooww way. I hastily finish the sentences of total strangers. He's a saver; I get rid of something the second it is no longer useful. He's patient; I rush. Sometimes when I'm working on a house project I need him with me to slow me down. I am a fast, impatient painter. He would sand the wood so far down, the molding wouldn't have any curves left. He's a stacker; I'm a filer. He claims to be organized in a funky, no-system way. I'm almost alphabetical. He's punctual; I'm late. He withers under stress; I thrive with some. He's a homebody; I'm social. He sees risk; I see opportunity. He's mechanically inept; I'm able.

This includes not knowing how to turn off the furnace or his car alarm. This became apparent one day when I heard a car alarm going off, but what was unusual was it kept getting louder and louder. I looked in the driveway, and there he was pulling in, all lights flashing, and horn blaring. He'd driven all the way home under these circumstances. Thank God for humor. It gets us through.

I was prepared for the feelings of first puppy-love and heart-beating infatuation to be replaced with a deeper, peaceful, content love. I guess what I wasn't prepared for was how that deeper love could sometimes be pushed aside by the white noise of life, the endless details and balancing acts that we all live each day. But simple kindness towards one another and showing respect to each other is the counter-balance to that white noise.

Marriage, for me, has been wonderful. It's incredible to think that you pick one person to share your whole life with, good times and bad. You have chosen each other, and you share intimacies that no one but the two of you know of. However, it does take effort. Mostly it takes time. It takes a commitment from both, and it takes communication.

I once heard that a successful marriage is 40/60. Both partners expect 40 percent, and both give 60 percent. A marriage transforms and takes many shapes through the years. One of the secrets to a successful marriage is accepting all the different shapes it takes and that each one is beautiful and challenging. You may not feel absolutely fulfilled by it each day, but realize that that is OK. So when you hear that car alarm coming down the street, just be glad that it's pulling into your driveway.

Jo Ann Stanley

Kung! Pao! So Yung! The disembodied face of my husband floats before me. Chop! Suey! Ouch! Fooey! His gorgeous blue eyes sparkle from behind wire-rimmed glasses. The salt and pepper hair—no, that's not right—he's older now and pepper-less—white wisps of hair straggle across the fair forehead as I punch! Jab! Kick! Knee! Forty minutes later, my husband, my marriage, and I have all survived kickboxing class.

I have no idea why my husband surfaced as my imagined opponent in kickboxing class, because in real life my husband and I rarely experience conflict with each other. We're a great team; we have a beautiful marriage. I cannot clearly remember ever having a serious argument since we were married, and that was seventeen years ago. Before our wedding, our only issues were whether to get married or not and whether we wanted kids or not. We finally took the plunge. In our married life we have discussions, differences, and occasionally some hurt or impatience, but rarely any anger. Generally we get along on issues big and small. Philosophically, we agree on politics, religion, most current events, and how to raise our children. We share our friends. We have a household management system that works for me: he spends most days at work and makes almost all of the money; I spend most days at home and spend almost all of the earnings. I write the checks, file the bills, go the grocery, clothe the children, and concoct the evening meal. Fortunately he has a great job, one he likes, and the money he makes is enough so that we don't run into conflict over finances. Neither of us is a spendthrift, nor a credit card junkie. Although we both consider ourselves feminists, our day-to-day chores are divided along more or less traditionally sexist lines: he does garbage; I do dishes. But when mom's away and dad must stay, or vice versa, either one of us can easily effect a crossover. At times, our priorities differ, but basically the only decision we have to revisit frequently is whose turn it is to walk the dog.

My marriage is my mainstay; I cannot imagine who I would be without it. My husband is my best friend: there is nothing I cannot share with him. My husband is my lover: our intimacy vital. My husband is my partner: what would parenting be without him? My husband mates my mind: what would any discussion, any issue, be without his input? What would reading a book mean to me if we did not discuss it? Day to day, night after night, year after year. . .my marriage makes me whole.

EXPECTATIONS

Releasing the Unrealistic

Consciously or unconsciously, you always get what you expect.

—Dr. Robert Anthony

Patricia Antonopoulos

*I*t is not the letting go that hurts; it is the holding on. . .Life is a constant seesaw of balancing expectations with reality. At times the balancing is as minor as equalizing the tiny plastic seesaw on which we place our baby, holding tightly to protect. Then there are those times when finding the symmetry feels like an unbearable weight from which we need protection.

Ripples on the pond preclude anyone's life from isolation. Our perfect outcome could wash over those closest to us with devastating results.

Why doesn't life work out according to expectations? It probably does, but not always to our personal expectations.

Certain events in our past are relegated to that place where we lock away the pain that would debilitate our daily lives. We expected a gift—a joy—and received so great a hurt that our 'light' was threatened. Our expectation was great and our reality, devastating.

What keeps the pain so throbbingly hurtful, lying just under the surface of this face we show the world?

At nineteen I married, and at twenty my son was born. In the delivery room, I was wild; pulling at the old leather wrist restraints that kept the woman out of the way so the medical people could do their work. I needed to touch my baby. His bloody, wailing, and thrashing little body was kept just out of my reach so that my need for my baby would not interfere.

When the nurse went to tell my husband that his son was born, they could not find him. He had grown tired of waiting. He left the hospital.

The birth of my five children closed ranks around the meaning of my life. My expectations were born in those life-defining moments.

As unfair as it was/is, they carried the expectations of my heart. A good mother doing all the happily-ever-after things was the expectation, was that light I cherished. The reality, the awareness of the diversity of expectation, threatened that light.

Heartache, heartbreak—theirs and mine—have chipped away the façade I created with my expectations. Assigning blame, realigning angers, searching for the right answer have not brought balance in the expectation/reality search.

It is not the letting go that hurts; it is the holding on. . .

Patti Dickinson

I was the parent of a sixteen-year-old runaway. She scorned our values. She scorned decency, anything Catholic, DARE, school, the preppie look, good judgment, algebra, meat. Everything.

She'd never been an easy kid. She followed what we now know to be an "expected, chronological, psychological pattern." At three-and-a-half, she was labeled Oppositional. In first grade, we added Attention Deficit Disorder. A little on the chunky side, she'd bound out of school, unaware that her backpack was spewing homework papers in the wind—littering the parking lot. By sixth grade, she was taking medication for depression. By seventh grade, she was angry, sullen and argumentative. By her sophomore year in high school, she was defiant and wrecking the structure of the family.

Junior year. Living with Elizabeth had become life with a loose cannon. Unpredictable. It'd been a halfway decent morning scene. Cereal, juice, the morning hustle of getting six school-bound kids where they needed to be, on time. She left with my husband Wood to go to Shawnee Mission North High School. It would be a week before we'd see her again. The School Resource Officer spotted her at North at the end of the week, and called us and the police, and she was transported to Juvenile Intake and then to Shawnee Mission Hospital. She needed to be evaluated. That bought us several night's sleep, and time to figure out what we were going to do with her. This time we got the grim diagnosis of bipolar disorder/manic depression. We made plans to send her to an Outdoor Wilderness School in Bend, Oregon. All the traditional psychological stuff had been tried; now we were doing something very offbeat and expensive. Not my style. All the paperwork in order, plane tickets purchased, and one more bump. Elizabeth ran, again, while outside for "recreation." This time she was gone for nineteen days.

I was paralyzed. Completely unprepared for the crushing numbness that became my existence for those many days. I was distracted, unable to concentrate on what anyone was saying. I was failing at what I was best at. Eye contact. Kindness. Reassurance. Hugs. Nurturing. I spent many days of this ordeal emotionally unavailable. Unprepared for the harsh exchanges that my husband and I were sharing too frequently, the clipped tones that we used with each other. We couldn't seem to get in sync. When he was quiet, distant, I was frightened by the silences we shared. I talked too much, questioned too much, wondered aloud too much. I was angry at his seeming passivity; likewise, he was weary of my talking it to death. I got meals on the table, enough clean underwear in the drawers and it became living by rote. Getting from here to there, but no real understanding or recollection of how that happened. A really lousy way to exist.

The dark road we walked taught me a handful of life lessons. That sometimes, despite my best efforts, there isn't a happy ending. But there were poignant, meaningful moments. From a seventh grade homemade Mother's Day card; "I just take all my anger out on you and that hurts you. Please don't let that spoil your happiness or anything on your Mother's Day." Written in residential treatment.

I've learned to trust my instincts. And learned, that until I have walked in someone's shoes, I'd better not judge nor have an opinion. And finally, that God writes straight with crooked lines.

Shawna Samuel

*E*xpectations. Yep, they can really screw some good things up. It seems that when you really look forward to something, it many times fails to live up to your lofty expectations. Yet many times when you are dreading something, it can end up being awfully fun.

I remember when I was a little girl, and I saved money for a little pirate-style telescope. When I finally got it, I felt nothing. I didn't feel the joy, happiness and utter contentment I was sure that little telescope would bring me; I didn't love it after all. How could that be?

But I remember being in K-Mart with my mother. I must have been about 7, desperately trying to choose between an orange and yellow plastic wheelbarrow and a set of large, plastic garden tools. I surely couldn't have both. Mom shocked me by saying that I could get them both. I still remember the exaltation I felt walking out of K-Mart that day. No nasty expectations to mess things up, for I thought we were there for shampoo and kitty litter.

Christmas, for me, has always been a very special, romantic time. For years when we were first married with children, I was consistently disappointed with the holidays. I think my expectations were so high, nothing could match them. Then the busy schedules of school events, invitations and increasingly longer do-lists would get in the way. I'd be exhausted and stressed which ruined the day. I'd envision the kids helping me make sugar cookies for hours and hours. I'd be disappointed when after a half hour they were tired and bored and off to another activity. Now I make a half recipe, and expect them to be involved for only a half hour. They love that time, as do I, but then they're out of there. It works. I do less, expect less, and receive more: more peace, more fun, more energy.

Expectations can really wreak havoc with the more important pieces of life, like expecting marriage to complete you forever. Expecting that the puppy love feelings will last forever, all day, every day can set anyone up for disappointment in a relationship. When I had my children, I expected to instantly love and know them, along with a full repertoire of lullabies and motherly advice. Expectations get in the way of a lot of joy for a lot of people. I have consciously made an effort to let go of expectations as much as possible and live in the moment. The number of ways it has helped, I cannot count. Even with the best of intentions, those expectations are stubborn and sly, sneaking in when you least expect them.

Jo Ann Stanley

When we were expecting our first, we nicknamed the fetus "Peapod." At the time we didn't know whether the baby was male or female. Soon amniocentesis confirmed our suspicions. By then "Peapod" was squirming in utero and we had no thought of changing her name until she was born. She developed a head like a hard little coconut, kicked occasionally over the months, then stopped kicking. With fear in our hearts we went to the doctor and learned that the baby was breech and the amniotic fluid very low. She was delivered by C-section a week in advance of her due date and we had no name fixed beyond "Peapod." It took three days to decide on her real name, Corinne.

When we were expecting our second, technology revealed her gender at only 12 weeks. So we knew more or less from the get-go that she was a girl, and we named her Brooke months before she was born, because by then we were "experienced" parents.

When children are born, we expect our parenting to come naturally, but it was never that way for me. It didn't help that my first baby had colic and cried for four months; all that time I felt that I must be doing something wrong. Whenever I went out with the baby, I was self-conscious. At the grocery store, I felt like everyone there was watching me, when really they were simply doing their grocery shopping. In the mall I felt absolutely ridiculous pushing the stroller while holding my child, but if she cried, I didn't want to leave her in the stroller. Now I know that everyone uses the stroller for packages. It seemed like the baby was constantly nursing and I needed privacy for nursing, so I didn't go many places for a year. But after that year, I began to relax. I am sure my second baby benefited from my learning curve.

As the child grows, so do our expectations. Both teachers and parents must have high expectations for the young, who will generally rise to the level we expect of them. We mold our children during those early formative years.

Eventually, however, it becomes necessary to allow the child the freedom to break the mold and discover his or her own directions. This will happen inevitably even if we resist it; wouldn't it be better to relax? Offer guidance and support, not rigidity? Right now, for example, I expect both of the girls to do well in school and to graduate from college. I have to remind myself that those are the same assumptions my parents had for my three siblings and me, but only one of us went straight through college.

As these adolescent years progress, the challenge for my husband and me will be the setting aside of our own expectations as the girls develop their own.

RESOLUTION

Life's a Marathon Not a Sprint

The trouble is that not enough people have come together
with firm determination
to live the things they say they believe.

—Eleanor Roosevelt

Patricia Antonopoulos

Resolution is a tribute word.

In *Undaunted Courage*, Stephen Ambrose used undaunted to mean resolute, a statement of great courage, determination, heart. His book about Lewis and Clark chronicles the resolute courage of men who recorded their early exploration of the United States. We marvel at their physical and emotional determination.

Our group of ordinary women began a very different journey of exploration when we gathered for a dual purpose. From the beginning, we talked of our book evolving from the strength and courage we resolved to share.

We also talked of many things that would not be part of our book.

We learned that we did become a safe place to unburden from whatever felt heavy at the moment. We could talk, laugh, cry and reassure one another in as many ways as our very different personalities offered. All this sharing of strength and courage was done before, during and after we investigated our current topic for writing.

Our learning did not stop there.

As we did the inevitable two-step, one forward, two back, we tiptoed often. We were purposeful, yet somehow fragile. We learned that the sharing of strength and courage was the easy part. Blending and refining our concepts for the book confirmed our individuality, and our resolve to cherish what we were building.

We discovered that a nod was not always a vote of confidence or acceptance of an opinion. We learned that each of us has strengths with which to polish some rough spots. We learned that differences were not always cleared with a single airing. We learned that what might be considered a personal strength was not always a group strength.

Our resolution continues to move us forward and allows us to grow as we increase in awareness of self and of this treasured relationship. Strength and courage are being explored on many new levels.

Resolution is a tribute word.

Patti Dickinson

You may give them your love,
but not your thoughts,
for they have their own thoughts.
You may house their bodies,
But not their souls,
For their souls dwell in the house of tomorrow,
which you cannot visit, even in your dreams.
—Kahlil Gibran

Resolution is an emotional compromise, a realization that not every ending will be a happy one and being able to walk away without leaving shreds of shattered expectations. Coming to terms. No longer being tortured by the "what ifs." Resolution means moving beyond replaying the facts over and over.

My struggle right now is dealing with one of my teenagers. I find myself trying to avoid conflict. I dodge the touchy areas, steer around the land mines. I negotiate the troubled waters, and in the process my integrity is diminished. It's like dealing all over again with a two-year-old. Unpredictable, governed by impulse, not able to compromise, give a little, get a little. The sources of the conflict are many—they blindside, emerge out of nowhere. I so cavalierly told friends that my attitude is that I am the parent; that is my role. It's not my job to be her friend. That the line between parenting and friendship needed to be kept apart or chaos would ensue. But a part of me yearns for a little of that kind of companionship.

Many for instances. Dillard's—shopping for swimsuits. She wanders away, meandering the aisles, picking out an armload of suits. Her body language speaks volumes. I point out a suit. "Hmmmm." Barely looks. Into the dressing room. One by one, I'm put in a position of saying, "Too small." "Too tight—you need the next size." All these comments, cordially spoken are met with silence or a straight-line mouth. Retreating to our separate corners. We head home, swimsuit-less. Driving with eyes straight ahead. This time my mouth is a straight line. Neither of us suggests an ice cream stop. The hostility is palpable. How did we get to this place? This is the daughter whom six months ago Wood and I spent every single Saturday watching cross the finish line at every single cross country meet. And she was so glad we were there. This rudeness, all this over a SWIMSUIT? Where is the anger coming from? Why the sullenness? I am afraid of her silence. I want to clear the air—I don't want her to stew. I dislike her pouting. I want her to know that I am uncomfortable with the silence, hostility.

We dance this dance over and over. With eye shadow, length of shorts, amount of time spent brushing her hair, her smart-aleck attitude about her algebra teacher. Shallow stuff. I tolerate it until I can't. The years go so fast—how did she get to be sixteen and so self-absorbed? I've got so little time left to make sure that all the things I wanted to instill are in place. I wasn't trying to instill the necessity of glitter. Or blue toenails, to match the blue of the t-shirt.

Maybe the silences remind me of the hostile silences my childhood was filled with. An angry mom. Sitting in the dimming light of a Sunday evening, watching "Wide World of Sports" and "The Ed Sullivan Show," drinking vodka and eating Lay's Potato Chips. I always marveled at how the group dynamic couldn't quite compensate for the chilly emotional climate of the room. What a powerful position she held. She could silence all of us with her icy presence— my Dad, my brother and I.

Silence still scares me—words are where the nurture and understanding begin.

Shawna Samuel

Resolution. What a complex word, fraught with meaning. In music, it can mean, simply, "the passing of a voice part from a dissonant to a consonant tone." To resolve something is to make it more pure, simpler. Resolve has a great deal to do with our success in life. To resolve issues in your heart simplifies your life. Life is a marathon, not a sprint. Endurance counts here. Think of all the different areas of life that benefit from resolution. Being married, raising children, doing well in a career. All will either succeed or fail based on our resolve.

When you marry, you resolve to commit your life, your effort, your loyalty and love to one partner. When you first hold your child in your arms you resolve to be a good parent. You simply try your best. You want to give them the best childhood you can with the best potential for a good future; and to let go when it's time. When you sign up for a job, whether it is salaried or volunteer, you resolve to do your best, to try your hardest.

Why is it then, for me, resolution sounds kind of bittersweet? It is a positive force in our lives, yet it can imply drudgery and mediocrity if you paint yourself into a corner with all of your resolutions. It also implies self-sacrifice, living with your mind and not your heart. As with everything in life, balance is important. Sometimes it is right to make a change. A resolution can be as simple as wanting to shed a few pounds (as if that's easy!), to making lifelong decisions.

I live much of my life guided by my resolutions. I hold myself to high expectations. I try to be a lot of things to a lot of people: a good wife, mother, friend, and granddaughter. I don't, very often, make decisions with my heart; many times it is guided by what the "right" decision should be. Is this a right or wrong way to live?

An area in my life that took great resolve was dealing with my grandmother, Veta. She was my grandmother on my father's side. Since my dad died when I was 11, she was my only link to him for the last 27 years, as I was for her. I am probably more like her than anyone else in the world. Sometimes I could show a simple mannerism, like touching my hair, and she would say that it gave her goose bumps because it seemed exactly like my father.

When I was born, my parents were still in college. She helped care for me during the days until I was four years old. I spent a great deal of time with her all through my early childhood. In all those years, I never, ever heard her raise her voice. She was the model of patience. Everything about her was gentle and kind. When I was five, we moved three hours away. When my family was packing up the car to drive away, I scooted over, patted the seat, and told her that she could sit by me. We lived far apart ever since. Even as a kid I would write letters to my grandparents asking them to move here so we could share each other's daily lives. Unfortunately, they never chose to do that. It wasn't until Veta was widowed, and had declined so much mentally that we had to move her here. We tried an apartment for a while, to give her a chance for independence, but it became quickly apparent that she couldn't do anything for herself anymore. She was diagnosed with Alzheimer's disease, and we had to place her in an assisted living apartment, the single most difficult decision my family has ever made.

I resolved to pay her back for all her patience and kindness she gave me when I was a child; and I learned that that was a big order to fill. Why is it that I wished for her daily involvement in my life always, and when I got it, she was literally losing her mind? When she moved up here, the movers were setting up her bed, and she told them to scoot it over to make room for my bed. Shadows of the past. When I told her that I wasn't sleeping there, but at my house, she said that she couldn't stay alone because she'd be too scared. I literally could not do enough for her. I could see her every day, and she wouldn't remember it, and she would depend on me more and more.

It took a great deal of resolve to call her, to share a twisted conversation of nonsense. It took a great deal of resolve to walk into her room, over and over again, many times with kids in tow, to clean up her bathroom, help her find things, take her out to lunch. Mostly it took resolve to not wish the time away, to not dream of the relief when her suffering was over, and maybe some of mine. And, once again, it took resolve to find a proper balance in doing enough for her, yet not letting the many other parts of my life suffer. I suppose that much of that resolve was an effort to avoid the inevitable guilt that has settled now that she's gone making me wonder if I did enough. How many of our actions are so motivated?

Resolve: to decide, to settle. A determination of will. Simple? Perhaps. Easy? Never. All I know is that it is a basic ingredient in me, and that for better or worse, I live by it, and put one foot in front of the other every day to walk this path I have laid out for myself.

Jo Ann Stanley

Resolution is all about making a promise to yourself and then breaking it. When I was a kid, all the resolutions I made were intended to reform my weak self into a better person: help mom more, get straight A's on my report card, stop playing in the creek (and avoid impetigo). As an adult, I've gotten out of the habit of making too many resolutions because I've learned they're way too hard to keep. Yet every New Year's Eve, heady with champagne, I decide there's got to be some behavior I can change. At this time in my life my resolutions have less to do with being a better person; instead, I want to be a younger one. The older I get, the more I am intent on reversing the aging process. At the same time I'm aware that there's no fountain of youth.

I decided to take my inspiration from my friend Marion, who at age 40 resolved to stick to elastic waistbands for the rest of her life. In Marion's view, middle age should reflect comfort and self-nurturing. Her approach includes bathtubs, hair dye, and Cabernet Sauvignon, not necessarily all together. So last year I resolved to pamper my nails. I was tired of being embarrassed by raggedy cuticles.

You know, the secret of keeping a resolution is to think small. Taking care of my nails seemed perfectly doable and desirable. I already owned a manicure kit, emery board, and nailbrush, but I went to the drugstore anyway and bought it all over again, adding cuticle cream, hand cream, rubber gloves, cotton gloves, gelatin capsules, nail hardener, nail polish and remover. I may have spent a fortune—never let be said that I make cheap resolutions—but please note, I didn't buy any artificial nails. I'm a nature girl. Then I made an appointment at Nail Perfection for the kick-off.

After a year, I patted myself on the back for keeping more than three manicure appointments at Nail Perfection, including at least two pedicures. Furthermore, I did my own nails at least once, and when I saw Marion over the summer she did them for me. Then why is it that today, as I tap these keys, they're as raggedy and scraggly as ever? What a high maintenance concept I had dragged myself into!

The tipping point came as I was huffing and puffing on the elliptical trainer, reading one of those "inspirational" beauty and fitness magazines. (Getting to the gym is one of those expired resolutions that I still revisit occasionally.) The author explained in gruesome detail how one can get horrible infections, fungi, chemical reactions, allergies, and, I might add, inferiority complexes, at nail and beauty salons almost anywhere in this great nation, not only in Hollywood. So keeping nails nice is actually a dangerous discipline! I trashed my resolution along with the magazine.

Speaking of the gym reminds me that this year's resolution is portion control. I've learned that a serving of chicken is the same size as a deck of cards, and an ounce of cheese is no larger than a smallish walnut. Fortunately I'm still ignorant of the proper guidelines for Hershey's Kisses. Half a bag? Three quarters?

UTOPIA

If I Could Change the World

Your passion is waiting for your courage to catch up.

—Marilyn Griest

Patricia Antonopoulos

With easy arrogance, I would wield the power for one year. No benign take-over cloaked with soft-spoken gentleness, but the will of an absolute dictator would be my rule of law. For 365 days, the changes would happen as I decreed.

First to suffer the swift sword of my reign would be the put-down, the smart remark, the verbal jousting that earns a touché for emotional harm. Any use of the gift of speech that produces "attitude" would be banned.

The Golden Rule stopped working years ago. Ignored, even ridiculed, that Rule has lost meaning. Now, with edict, all forms of stealing would end. The best of us could be given, but nothing would be allowed to diminish the value of another person. Worth could not be taken from another's life.

And accountability would be required of each day. To accomplish this I would change the life patterns we have formed by our worship of the god called Fun.

Our children are being trained to believe that Fun is the defining concept. School, church, work, sports, and holidays have all been enchanted by the spell of Fun. "Did you have fun?" is the universal question. Huge amounts of time, energy and money go into making life Fun for our children.

We give R rated movies to anyone over the age of 17. We give MTV to anyone with access to a television set. We give PG13 to any child, beginning with toddlers. We allow outrageous behaviors at parties in the guise of honoring Fun.

Our worship of entertainment has taught our children to embrace the outrageous. How easily we could have taught honor and respect.

During my year of power, commercial media would produce programs modeling the dignity of all people. . . no exceptions.

The joy and work of learning have languished under the spell of Fun. School days that are not Fun are not well tolerated. Learning must be fun or the schools are deemed inadequate.

How unfair. How sad. How deceptive.

In my land of enchantment, children would be taught to treasure doing the right thing with right defined as: principled, truthful, rational and loving.

My Kingdom for a Year would revel in Joy. Joy in family, in play, in accomplishment, in work, in success, in understanding. And to further this, I would decree that no mother or father be allowed to abandon the role of parent to assume the role of friend to his or her child. Pampering and excusing would disappear. Discipline, to make a disciple of, would be cherishing our children.

Of course, this life in my happy-ever-after months would refuse to give way at the end of my year . . .like that song that never ends, this arcadia goes on and on.

If I could change the world. . .

I cannot, and without future-vision, I probably would not.

We have created the social and cultural world we wanted. We have chosen the issues. Perhaps by well-intentioned people doing nothing. Perhaps by majority consensus. Perhaps by benign neglect, but we do live in the world that we created.

Patti Dickinson

*J*f I could change the world . . .
   Candy corn would be a vegetable
There would be no death row.

No unwanted children
No kid growing up in the foster care system
Abortion would be illegal
Everyone would feel compassion for the mentally ill and the homeless.

We would care as much about understanding as we do about being understood
We would treat this planet gently
Zoos would be simulated habitats, not cages for viewing convenience
We wouldn't feel complacent about what we read on the front page
   of the newspaper
It would be required that every kid experience one big blizzard
Nice guys would finish first every single time
And everyone would believe that kindness matters and live like they believed it.

We all would feel outrage when a kid is bullied on the playground,
   or a kid's picture is staring back at us from the milk carton as we
   eat our corn flakes
Smiling at strangers would be second nature
No one would be getting his next meal out of a trash can, or sleeping
   in a cardboard box
The Internet would clean up its act
We wouldn't have to legislate "No Child Left Behind"
Everyone would have a minimum of one belly laugh daily.

All four wheels on the grocery cart would go in the same direction
Righteous indignation would be our reaction to nighttime television
    and the movie industry
The village concept would work, every single time
We would recognize that sticks, stones and words are all capable of
    maiming the spirit in equal measure
We would reexamine gently, our long-held tired beliefs: two-year-olds
    are impossible, teenagers, blacks, liberals, conservatives, the poor, the rich,
    the government . . .
We would fill the front page of the newspaper with examples of how
    the human spirit can triumph.

More of us would pay it forward
Fragile and resilient would co-exist within each and every human being.

Shawna Samuel

My child came home from school last week, upset that the whole class missed recess because two kids didn't stop talking through math. I had to explain that the group does suffer for the actions of a few, in school, and in life. He said that he didn't think that was fair. It's not. When I started thinking of examples to give, I realized how invasive that reality is in our society. Think about airport security. Think of all the innocent people who have hours of their lives stolen because they have to be searched, frisked and x-rayed. God forbid you forget for a minute and pack nail clippers in your purse. Those will be thrown away at the gate. How about milk cartons and medicine bottles that are sealed securely enough to withstand a nuclear blast just because some bloke put arsenic in Tylenol 25 years ago. Do you ever wonder what some old person with arthritis has to go through just to down a couple of Tylenol with a glass of milk?

It's quite a day when people are honored and called heroes for turning in a billfold they found with cash in it. Or how about when you send your son to a baseball game with a water bottle, and he has to throw it away at the gate because they are suspicious that it might contain alcohol. So instead you spend twenty bucks on Cokes. Imagine the expense of all of the shoplifting preventions that are in stores. And have you ever purchased a sweater and had to trudge back to the store to have the sensor removed because they forgot it? I have.

We recently took our children to visit Washington D.C. and were saddened by the intense security. Each museum and office building has long lines outside because each person must go through magnetic sensors, and have his or her bags searched. There are men with machine guns and binoculars on buildings around the National Mall. You cannot drive by the White House any longer. And all of the buildings, all of them, are surrounded by barricades of giant concrete slabs or the more updated heavy concrete planters that are scattered every 18 inches. All this so that nobody can drive a car with a bomb in it up to a building. When they are searching my teenage daughter's backpack, and she looks at me like she's humiliated, is she paying the price or are they? What has she done to deserve this? I ask you, has terrorism won?

So if I could change the world, I'd make the actions of the many good-hearted, honest people the ruling force, not the actions of the few bad ones. And I'd like to be able to show my children every day how the good in the world far out-weighs the bad.

Jo Ann Stanley

I I could change the world, there would be no more human suffering. No pain, disease, war, abuse, or hunger. No pimples, boils, or pus. No slugs or slime. No menstrual cramps. No dog hair in the carpet. In my Utopia husbands would not go out of town for business. Adolescence would be abolished. Fat and calories would be historic concepts. And 9/11 would never have happened.

On my planet, Nature retains all her glory. Pansy, daffodil, iris and orchid bloom together in wild abandon, sun or shade. Each snowflake stays unique; each autumn leaf provides its blaze of color; each firefly sparks the July night. The double helix of DNA spins its secret code and babes are born, but they are never blind or stunted. There won't be crippling disabilities or even high-functioning labels like "Asperger's Syndrome." Instead there might be benign, uncomplicated conditions, such as "Asparagus Syndrome": the tendency to overeat a certain green stalky vegetable, and the smell of human urine after eating it.

At the beach, the sun still sinks in an orange-purple sky as green phosphorescence lights up the surf. Guess what? Kansas would be a beach. No, I take that back. Here in Kansas we will always have prairie grass, a limitless horizon, and a blue umbrella sky, but Dorothy and Toto would hail from Oklahoma and Topeka would become an emerald destination. In Topeka, you would find shopping, nightlife, gourmet restaurants, innovative architecture, and world-class museums. It would be like Chicago. From Topeka, Route 70 will still cross the state. At 3:00 in the morning, when you stop your innovative pollution-free super fast vehicle halfway to Colorado, you will still see a trillion stars sparkling overhead. We Kansans will continue to ski in Colorado, because there the Rockies scrape the sky and the adrenaline rush of cascading down the mountain makes you feel like a fish in a waterfall.

People in my universe will possess brilliant imaginations, amazing artistic, musical, and literary talent, a superb sense of humor, and a dramatic zest for life. Kindness will be the sixth sense; beauty will flow from kindness. There will still be children, innocence, laughter, and song. As in Star Trek, a teleportation device instantly beams us up anywhere we want to go. Little Red Riding Hood could pop over to see her (healthy) grandma whenever she wanted even if the old lady lived on the moon. The wolf might be lost in forest or meadow, but even he would be happy. Books and better babysitters will be plentiful and free. Out with Atkins', in with Pierpont's; heady white wine; warm freshly baked rolls with olive oil for dipping; macadamia encrusted salmon; a salad of field greens with pears, spiced walnuts, and gorgonzola; crème brûlée, or as a healthy point exchange alternative, chocolate mousse. Scintillating conversation would dominate not only at trendy restaurants but also in our homes, at our kitchen tables, where little kids would quit bickering and even teens would fill us in on their lives.

My world could never be a "brave new world." We wouldn't want to drug ourselves with Soma, or TV, or Game Boy. There would still be infinite variety and countless grains of sand. Love, awe, and curiosity would remain intact at the expense of anger, hate, and stupidity. "Big Brother" would be a clumsy bear in red hat and yellow raincoat, perfectly harmless. Orwell's terrifying "Room 101" would instead be a luxury suite overlooking the sea with sheer white curtains flowing onto the balcony. A mosquito net would drift over the bed but no mosquitoes would be buzzing, and if I were to ring room service for champagne, I would discover that they've hired my husband as the oversexed bellhop. But wait—this job has to have strict parameters—the only room he ever visits is mine.

If I could change the world, there would be peace on earth. Politics would be passé. Neither religion nor ethnicity would be issues: differences and diversity would be sources of celebration. If I could change the world, there might be death, but it would never be painful or premature. No freak accidents; no car accidents. Death would be like falling asleep and arriving in a world of dreams, never nightmares. Yes, heaven; no, hell. If I could change the world, the spiritual plane would fly close enough for more of us to get on board. For this trip you could fly without a passport and you wouldn't even have to pass through security. You could leave your shoes on your feet and your grandmother's manicure scissors in your purse. You'd have the opportunity to visit with loved ones and revel in their comfort. Rather than ignoring your mother's advice the way you did when she was alive, you could tell her how much you appreciate everything she ever said.

Even if I could change the world, there is one special thing I would never change or exchange: this incredible, wonderful life that I lead, with every privilege, with loving family, brilliant children, beautiful friendships, and a Golden Retriever named Topaz.

FRACTURED SLEEP

What Keeps Me Awake at Night

If the world were merely seductive, that would be easy.
If it were merely challenging, that would be no problem.
But I arise in the morning torn between a desire to improve (or save) the world
and a desire to enjoy (or savor) the world.
This makes it hard to plan the day.

—E.B. White

Patricia Antonopoulos

Selfishness, anger and the need to direct what isn't mine to control are my big three when it comes to those tossing and turning nights when the brain refuses to settle into sleep. Ironically, much of this wakefulness is a ramble in the past, endlessly sorting what cannot be changed.

The evil twins of anger and control can wrap those blankets into knots more quickly than a thousand blinks of crying eyes.

Each of us has debts of obligation, promises assumed by relationships in marriage, parenting, employment, friendships and community. Learning that fulfilling obligations does not automatically guarantee control is a most difficult lesson. True control usually ends with the limits of self-control.

Anger, voiced or silent, can have me punching a pillow at 2:00 a.m. That anger often results from the need to control the past actions of another person, an amazingly non-productive night's work.

Selfishness grows ugly when the secret heart wants appreciation for what voice and demeanor describe as "just routine—no thanks necessary."

Believing and teaching that appreciation and acknowledgement are not necessary places the burden of mind-reading on the backs of loved ones. Family members are expected to intuitively understand when there is a need for appreciation.

"Be a light unto yourself" is attributed to Buddha. Perhaps self-light is looking at the essence of anger and the limits of control. . . unimpeachable obligations to those with whom we share this life.

Patti Dickinson

Wondering what keeps my kids awake at night.

While I have learned to love Elizabeth differently, I still get a lump in my throat at the mention of the Kansas City Art Institute, or when I walk by the Fairway Frame Shop and see some up-and-coming artist's stuff in the window.

Wondering what I've missed. What conversations I didn't have that I should have, what conversations I did have that I should have simply left well enough alone.

The could have, should have, might have beens.

Wondering if I've given my kids the right model of how it's done and then getting honest enough to voice that I haven't always modeled what I was trying to teach.

Knowing that I don't have all the answers, and worrying that an awful lot of people think I do.

In the middle of the night, just about anything is fair game:

Who needs to floss more,

Who needs me to recognize them for something unacknowledged,

If Mary Morgan and that birth order book are right about middle kids,

Who needs a lunch for a field trip (and there's no bread),

Who needs their bangs trimmed,

A wart removed,

Whose winter coat is too small,

Who's getting a raw deal on the playground,

Who needs one more stern reminder about chewing with their mouth closed, leaving an empty toilet paper roll on the holder or forgetting a soggy washcloth on the shower floor,

Who needs some work on being a better loser, and who needs to tone down the gloating when they win.

That all my kids don't, on any given day, need me in equal measure, and I hope my kids aren't keeping score. Some of my kids have a credit, and some of them won't LIVE long enough for me to equalize the time I've spent worrying about them. I hope that they know that I don't have a mental balance sheet.

I hope, when all is said and done, that the benefits of large families outweigh the shortfall of time, energy and resources.

What I said, and shouldn't have.

What I should have said and didn't.

How I have loved every single step of raising kids (sometimes in hindsight), and I grieve the passing of those stages.

Are my kids independent enough, generous enough, smart enough, competitive enough, savvy enough, confident enough, grateful enough, Godly enough?

If Claire really thinks that a checking account balance of $1.81 three months in a row is "managing her money"?

Teachable moments that I missed—completely.

That Mary Morgan laughingly calls herself "Chip"—as she looks across the room and nods in my direction and says, "Yeah, I'm a chip off the Young Block." She's given me big shoes to fill.

The pressures and decisions that I know my high school kids face—in the hallways, on the weekends.

That my kids think going to the grocery store with me—solo—is quality time.

That there's not enough of me to go around.

That I won't remember how to slow down when I have time to do that.

That Matt might not know that even at those times when we were both at our worst, I still loved him unfailingly.

What a marriage without kids living in the house will be like.

This frenetic mental search for evidence that our civilization isn't on the downhill side of its decline.

That the legacy I leave my children is an example of moral courage and sturdiness.

Shawna Samuel

*H*ere's the deal. I'm married to someone who has never particularly enjoyed the corporate world. He has forced himself, day after day, to get up and participate in that world. He's always had good jobs in his field, but has not always had good luck. He's lost his job twice, in buyouts, downsizings, etc. Now he has risen to a place appropriate for his age and experience, but where he's totally outside his comfort zone. And he wants out. He's 57 years old, and he wants out for good. Retirement. Now.

I, on the other hand, have always embraced the corporate world. I have loved every job I've ever had. Anyone who truly knows me thinks I have a career ahead of me. It was a tremendous sacrifice for me to stay at home to raise children. In fact, one of the appealing things about marrying Duncan was that he was willing to be the stay-at-home parent so I could have a career. I'm not sure why that never happened. I suppose those babies are a little more intimidating to a father when they actually arrive. And men don't have breasts, the major draw for a newborn. Now, 16 years into it, I'm preparing to go back to that career world, so he can get out of it. We've never had fancy cars, or enjoyed luxurious vacations, we don't feel we can add on to our home, and wonder what college expenses will do to us. However, we're both happy with our level of success, happy with our choices. And both feel it was absolutely worth material sacrifices to have a parent at home all these years.

In many ways, I am more than ready to go back to work. I feel in my heart, I will thrive with that stimulation again. I don't feel I was ever really meant to stay at home for so long; but here's the rub, now that I have, I'm afraid I've lost my edge. You know: the competitive player who can jockey for position out there in the "real world." And there are all these huge expectations for me. I shouldn't just get a job; it should be a career. My family is waiting for me to light the world on fire, when today, I'm really pretty happy changing the sheets and getting dinner ready. Plus, I don't know which direction I should turn. There are so many different jobs I would like. Should I go back to some of my old contacts? Should I try a new path? How does someone begin when they've been away for so long? And how do you leave the world that you know, with the comforts of the same people, and the freedom to make a day your own? It feels claustrophobic to think of having to be somewhere, maybe even somewhere without a window, from 8:00 to 6:00 every single day. But Duncan has never had the choice, so why should I?

And I can lie awake and worry that things around our house won't run the way I like them to run. I'm afraid that Duncan won't do many of the things that I like done and I'll end up having to do it all. I'm afraid I'll resent him for wanting out, pushing me back in when I'm almost at the finish line with my children. I'm afraid of growing apart from the kids, not being the one to be here if they are home sick. Not being the one to walk Alex home every day. Not being—well—The One. And I'm feeling the pressure that surely every dad out there feels, of not being able to earn enough money to do right by them all. The fear of messing up, of letting them down is great. But why should that pressure belong to the man alone? It takes so much money to live today.

I also feel that I've fallen into a peach of a job with the city clerk position. It is perfectly tailored for me. I have the flexibility my family needs, and feel I do a good job for the city. I really have things in shape and running smoothly, so I hate to turn my back on such a good thing. But could I do both? How much of a super-woman am I going to try to be?

Yet it seems a change needs to happen soon. It is stressful living with someone who is unhappy. I feel sorry for him. I've tried the "look on the bright side" comments, and he finally told me that they just don't help, and he'd appreciate it if I'd stop. He hates his job, and it would help him if I'd hate it too. He feels like he is losing his true self to this job. He finally told me not to ask him how is day was when he comes home at night; that there is never a good answer to that question. It is terrible to live with someone who feels that way. I've never before had the actions and feelings of another individual so directly related to my everyday life and what it will be like. That is stress. And that is what keeps me awake at night.

Jo Ann Stanley

What keeps me awake at night? Caffeine. That late night cup of coffee. Or worse, a completely indulgent evening with fine wine, creamy food, a decadent chocolate mousse, and espresso, if not cappuccino.

What do I think about when I wake up at 3:00 a.m., tossing and turning? Honestly, for the first thirty minutes or so, I stew about the fact that after all that rich food and drink, I've got to get up to use the bathroom. I wait as long as I can. After that's out of the way, my mind spins and spins, sometimes for hours. I obsessively replay the day with all my worst mistakes. What happened? Why did I say that? Why didn't I bite my tongue?

The bottom line is that I'm really a very insecure person when it comes to interpersonal relations. I often worry that peope don't really like me. I have a bad habit: I speak before I think. I'm critical, and I've been criticized for being too blunt. I fully identify with my zodiac sign, Aries, the ram-head down, with horns, forceful. On the surface, in a meeting, or in a professional setting I seem like I'm ultra-confident. By day I have many wonderful friends, and I feel good about myself. But at home, in the dark, especially when my husband is traveling, I sometimes feel sad and alone. I'm trying to live morally and responsibly; I try to give my best to those I love and to all those I meet. But when I'm alone at night, I'm like an abandoned child. Like the child, I blame myself and feel rejected.

When I was a young girl, my older brother forced me to watch a movie that terrified me. He locked the door and wouldn't let me leave until the horror flick was over. The film was called "Fingers at the Window," and to this day I'm traumatized by that image: the hands tapping at the glass. For many years, at night, when I was physically alone, the image would come back to me and every creak in the house would frighten me. I'd fear going down to the basement, yet I couldn't sleep until I'd explored every inch of the house, even the closets and the garage. Even afterwards, I was afraid that someone would sneak into the house in the middle of the night and attack me.

After I was married, and especially after I had children, this fear seemed to leave me. Maybe there was so much noise in the house I didn't hear the small creaks. Dog, cat, and kids kept me company when my husband was away on business. Somehow being in the role of protector took away my own fear. I knew I would do anything to rescue those toddlers from an intruder, and somehow, that made me brave.

Now that my children are adolescents, my fears more often center on them. They are so young, so beautiful; that in itself makes them weirdo magnets. Not exactly naïve, my teenage daughters nonetheless seem very vulnerable. So there are nights when I lie awake thinking about what will happen to them and fearing for their futures. I worry about the risks they'll take and the mistakes they'll make.

There are times too, that I worry about my husband. Sometimes when he's away, I can't help thinking that he'll be in an accident or in a plane crash, and I'll get that phone call. When he was training on his bicycle for MS 150 rides, I was afraid he'd be hit by a car. Occasionally I wonder what would happen to us if he ever lost his job. My greatest fear is how I could ever go on without him.

Guilt. Guilt can keep me awake at night. Now that I'm the mom, I can't help feeling guilty about the many sleepless nights I must have given my own mother. I feel guilty about all the mistakes I've made raising my kids. I feel guilty about all the little nit-picking goof-ups I've made each day, and all too often, some larger, more significant error. Thank goodness that most nights I skip the coffee and sleep like a rock.

PAST HURTS

A Sore Place in the Spirit

If we had no winter, the spring would not be so pleasant.
If we did not sometimes taste of adversity, prosperity would not be so welcome.

—Anne Bradstreet

Patricia Antonopoulos

Someone once told me that it is possible to understand oneself by examining early memories . . . going back to formative circumstances to clarify the self-portrait.

This idea feels like an octopus caught in a spider web.

My parents had a close friend, Father John, a Catholic priest. His parish was a small church community, the site of many family overnights. Dad, my brothers and Father John would hunt; Mom, my sisters and I cleaned the rectory and played on the parish grounds.

In the country air we worked with determination and played with abandon. After the traditional spaghetti dinner, we slept deeply.

The girls had quilt pallets on the upper level. My spot was near the stairs so I could protect my sisters from a fall.

Awakening was slow and confused. Suddenly, I could not have remembered ever sleeping. Panic was as total as the darkness. An adult male was touching me and saying,

"Don't speak. Don't move. Go back to sleep, Patty Ann."

Two people called me Patty Ann—my Dad and Father John.

There is no clear memory of how long it took me to tell my parents, but the memory of their response is totally clear.

I had been dreaming.

End of discussion, end of emotional security.

Later I talked to our parish priest in the confessional. His response was to ask me what I had done to create the situation. How had I caused the priest to touch my 12-year-old body as I slept?

End of trust.

What was done to me physically was unforgivable—is unforgivable. Accepting the gentle touches of family and friends took a very long time, and can still be difficult.

What was done to me emotionally might easily be hung on societal and religious beliefs. Priests were above reproach, protected by custom, honored by the unwavering dedication of church members.

Understanding that rationale as it fit in time and circumstance enables me to accept my parents' response for what it was.

But the ramifications of that incident are the tentacles of the octopus, reaching every part of my life. The web is my protection, my barrier against that pain, my sore place in the spirit.

Patti Dickinson

*I*n our bedroom, we have a full wall of bookcases. Wood and I are both avid readers and cannot resist the bookstore's lure on many of our Saturday evenings. We are never, ever in the same section of the bookstore. So we usually spend the first hour of our date apart. He's in science fiction, film, computers, magazines or looking for a music CD. Eclectic in his musical taste. I am in memoirs, self-help, true crime, non-fiction, and NOT where he is, looking for music CDs. I am stuck in the seventies. Greatest hits genre. Moody Blues, Beatles. Neil Diamond. Way stuck.

Over the years, there has not been much observable rhyme or reason to the way that our books are organized. And in recent months, since we are running out of room, books are put wherever they fit. Not necessarily spine out, tilt-your-head-to-the-right to read the title. Certainly no Dewey decimal mentality. In fact there isn't even a fiction/non-fiction mentality. Yesterday was the day. I took eight shelves, one-third of the available space and emptied them out. On the floor, on the bed, on the table, temporarily in the arms of a kid that just happened to be walking by—didn't matter. Organizing had begun. 409 cleaner and TWO rolls of paper towels. Dust everywhere. Hair in a ponytail, sleeves rolled up. Coughing, sputtering, sucking in dust bunnies, but definitely a woman on a mission. You know the look.

The beginnings of order. Fiction and non-fiction. About evenly divided. More stability than our book collection had EVER seen. Found the folder from the pancake breakfast from last year. Found Navy letters. Found the Shawnee Mission North Directory. The one I'd used to make pleading, frantic call after call, looking for Elizabeth when she ran away. A spiral notebook full of her poetry, journaling, drawing. Angry stuff. Read in an attempt to know who this stranger was that had been sharing the same living space for seventeen years. Would never have guessed that my daughter could write such spitting, angry words. Anger at everyone and everything. Middle of the night silent screaming called writing. Piercing, shrill. Pieces of a life well lived, pieces of a life with a few scabs, pieces of a not-all-sorted-life.

Now I know why I haven't begun this project. Embarking on this big cleaning mission requires that I find a home for a lot of miscellany that decorates this bookshelf. Because if it already had a place to be, it would be there.

My current, albeit rare, conversations with Elizabeth never organize themselves around feelings. Rather, the organizational themes are rarely things we agree on. Somehow the questions I can't ask are replaced with questions that will evoke feelings in her. Okay, pushing buttons. School, overdue Blockbuster stuff. A bounced check to QuikTrip. Don't really know what my motivation is. I guess I want her to express some of her feelings out loud. To perhaps see what will elicit the feelings that mean she's still connected. To fill the silences and stop the fluff. Who wants bus stop talk that you'd have with strangers with their own kid? Our conversations are littered with stilted chatter and awkward silences.

I know I could be more forgiving with other peoples' kids. Lots of families have kids that drift for a time. But the rub is that Elizabeth's drifting is not purposeful. She isn't making the choice to drift. It's the horrific reality of a mental illness that defies understanding. It is. And nothing can change that. The unrelenting grip of a disease that will never, ever, let go. I cannot imagine I will ever get to acceptance. Conceding is giving up. I cannot seem to get beyond the crippling sadness of it.

For both of us.

Shawna Samuel

eath is so final, yet grieving is certainly not. When I was 11 and my father was 32, he was camping over a weekend. He was in his bass boat about 10:00 at night setting a trout line when a drunk driver in a much larger boat went speeding directly through his boat, killing him. That's the short story. The long story is that my spirit never healed because I never grieved. The memories I have of that time are not of my loss, but of everyone else's. It was traumatic for me to see my grandfather weep. It was traumatic for me to see my mother paralyzed by grief, literally for years after his death. It was even difficult to see the yellow lab, my dad's dog, stop waiting for him by the door every night at 5:00. How could I cry? How could I add to their problems? In my childish eyes they were obviously not strong enough to handle my real feelings, so I canned them and coped.

Besides, at age 11, you don't comprehend your own personal loss, you just navigate through the depths of the grief surrounding you that fill your day. You find a way to make things better. For me, I got busy cleaning the kitchen, putting away all the food that was pouring into our house. I took meticulous care of our houseplants, nurturing them like I suppose I wished to be nurtured. One of my best friends brought me a new kitten to help with my grief. What a lovely gesture. I put my heart and soul into caring for him. What's weird is, as I look back on that time, I never really liked that cat. And for anyone who knows me at all, that is strange. I remember the day of my dad's funeral, I spilled a small glass of Coke, and I went nuts. I was so mad at myself, cried, yelled. But I was just told that it wasn't any big deal, my dress would clean. Didn't they see?

At age 11 you also worry excessively about what your peers are going to think about you now that you are different. They didn't know what to say to me, so they said nothing. They didn't come around, or reach out. He died in July, so I was totally isolated until school started, at which time my worry was so intense, I dreaded even walking in the door. Those, I think, were the things occupying my mind, keeping me from my grief. And when you don't go through the grief, you live it over and over again throughout your life.

They called my mom at midnight on July 13th to tell her that my dad's boat was found circling, empty on the lake, in high gear. He'd obviously tried to get out of the way, but they couldn't find him. They didn't find him for three days. I remember seeing my mom in my room several times during that night, and sensing that something was wrong. When I awoke, neighbors and friends were gathered around her downstairs. I took forever brushing my teeth, my hair, making my bed. I had a long, long ponytail, wore glasses and was wearing white t-shirt with an apple on it that said "I like you", with a big bite out of the apple. My mom came upstairs and told me that my dad had been in an accident, and that she really needed me now. In an instant I was transformed into the strong one. If she'd only said, "Your dad's been in an accident, but we'll get through this, one way or another. I'm here for you, I'm sad but I'm strong, just let it go, lean on me..." Then my spirit wouldn't be so sore.

Jo Ann Stanley

Sore place in the spirit: ache of regret, gaping wound.

Red oozing tissue. Bruise gone black,
to blue,
to spidery brown.

The mistakes made. The times wronged or wrong.
Beyond. . . that sore place in the spirit.. . lie holes in the heart.
A miscarriage. An illness. Pain, disease, disability. Abuse. Death.

Death: loss.
    the loss of a friend,
    a sibling,
    a parent,
    a spouse.

A mother's grief for her child!
A sore place in the spirit will never heal completely.

But without pain, we could not know joy.
Without a sore place in the spirit, our spirits would not, could not, soar.

SEASONS OF GRATITUDE

Life is Happening

I think it pisses God off
if you walk by the color purple in a field somewhere—
and don't notice it.
—Alice Walker, *The Color Purple*

Patricia Antonopoulos

Maybe a lifelong sense that every day is one of joy begins with early memories. When I began to think and write about Seasons of Gratitude, my snapshot memories were primarily of those years when my children were young.

The scent of orange peel awakens childhood Christmas and memories built on the support of family.

A failed catalytic converter invokes teen memories, driving around Wyandotte County Lake, relishing the gasoline fumes from that first set of wheels.

Iced bourbon means Dad is close by.

Butter melting in warm milk is Dad again. When the time between payday stretched too long, Dad made his specialty, cracker soup. Warm milk, butter and broken soda crackers were transformed into a dinner time event.

Incense unlocks a time of innocence when my church was perfect and an angel named Patrick guarded day and night.

Ivory soap brings my babies home again, feeling their weight, inhaling their new life smell, feeling their protective shield—my arms.

Chocolate chip cookie dough puts my five, and a few neighbor kids, around the kitchen table, spoons at the ready, hoping I will say they may eat half the dough before baking.

Fresh grass clippings and wood smoke welcome the hours into years spent with my children, Mark, Elizabeth, Paul, Dan and Chris, playing in Swope Park, a place my grandfather taught me to love.

Chalk dust and finger-paint never fail to revisit, with gratitude, the joys of teaching.

Desitin and baby powder totally fill my joy world because my grandchildren, Cain, Molly, Frank and Sam are born again, allowing me to retrace the wonders of their becoming.

Diesel fuel and train grease signal the end of Bob's workday and the beginning of our evenings together.

Contrast forms gratitude. If the glass is always empty or full, we have less to appreciate.

Lysol is sadness. Michael, much-loved brother-in-law, is home from Viet Nam via Walter Reed Army Hospital. He is sick with some unknown illness, and the newborn Chris must be protected. Everything near Mike gets tainted with the smell of Lysol.

Hospital smell means that my Dad must die yet another lingering death.

Urine made sickeningly sweet by an overlay of cinnamon freshener will always put Mom back behind the locked door the of dementia wing.

Our youngest son, Chris, has a thing he says. "It's all good." At this moment, his wisdom feels just right.

Shoveling out after a snowstorm makes the warm cup all the sweeter.

Bacon is Sunday morning after church, growing up on Tauromee Ave.

Lemon meringue pie and hot coffee taste like Pop Smith teasing about my inability to brew coffee at just the right sipping temperature.

Biscuits and homemade grape jam are Easter at Mom's table.

Fried chicken dinners or lasagna mean that my children are gathered around the kitchen table in Fairway, Kansas.

And frogs. And socks.

And pewter hearts.

But especially frogs of all shapes, sizes and colors are my link to a unique friendship, that perfect exception to friendships of circumstance. Together my friend and I have walked a common ground, listening, accepting, encouraging, guiding and gently redirecting when needed.

Family photos, the history of smiles and tears, eyes and heart filed with the sight of a family growing and changing, moving away physically but becoming more entrenched emotionally, the quiet presence of daughters-in-law, Kaiya, Ida and Kristi enriching our family with their grace and beauty. These are the unforgettable markers for gratitude, my reasons to celebrate, my greatest joys.

Patti Dickinson

Thirty years is time enough
    To bring eight kids into our home after four miscarriages
Live in three apartments in three different cities
Collect a menagerie of three cats, two bunnies, a snake,
        gerbils, a series of hermit crabs
Travel to Romania
Lose a son to confusion
And a daughter to bipolar disorder
To deliver that first home-grown baby in a thunderstorm
Time enough to add two Eagle Scouts to the planet,
One Tim Griggs, one Golden Ruler, one Ursuline finalist.
One #17 heptathlete in the nation, one kid with the curliest hair
        and a curly-que kid e-mail address,
        a stand-up comic
        and that #8 baby that will be CEO of something
Time enough to spend more than fifteen years at Cape Cod, collecting
        well-worn driftwood
Time enough to be resilient and fragile. Time enough to have seen
        each other's defeats and triumphs, time enough for some regrets.
But time enough for much contentment.
Time enough to be sure
        that I want to stay with you.
To acknowledge our humanity
And profess our belief in the God that united us to save what we can't,
        by ourselves.
Time enough to learn that a broken heart still beats,
        and maybe, heal itself.
Time enough to put a front porch on the house where we will block
        the rest of our lives.

Shawna Samuel

There are decidedly two ways to look at things: the bright side and the dark side. Usually both exist in any situation. I am fortunate—I nearly always see the bright side. Nearly. It is a gift, the gift of appreciation. I believe it comes naturally for me for several reasons.

One, my husband is 16 years older than I. Recently I returned to full-time work after being at home with my children for 17 years. When I left the professional world to raise our children, I was 25. These years have flown by, and now, as I work with 25-year-olds who feel that they're immortal, I want to say to them, "I was your age about ten minutes ago." I would say it if it wouldn't be the final definitive sign that I was, indeed, old.

Being able to be at home with my children for 17 years before becoming a working mom is my greatest blessing. We've sacrificed material possessions to have a parent at home, but we've never been sorry. To have life slow to the pace of a baby and a toddler is a wonderful and fleeting gift.

When I stopped working, my husband was the age that I am now. And in that same blink of 17 years, he's 61. Won't I be that age in an equal flash? My father, a healthy 31-year-old left to go fishing one weekend and never returned due to a fatal accident. I've now lived more than a dozen years longer than he had the opportunity to live. How could I not appreciate each day?

I have friends who have traversed horrible tragedy. One has buried a three-year old daughter to cancer. One is fighting cancer herself. She dreams of having a day where she gets to go to work, gets to cook dinner for her family and gets to put the kids to bed. What a weighty difference there is in "gets to" rather than "has to." People make it through these challenges, albeit changed, but what choice is there? As my grandmother would say, "We play the hand we're dealt."

When I get in my car to leave for work each day, I can feel sorry for myself that I'm not at home doing what I want to do with my family, or I can be grateful that I have a second family I work with whom I respect, learn from and enjoy. Having been away from the professional world for 17 years, I appreciate that opportunity and see the fun in it. There are times I want to look at everyone in a meeting and say, "Do you know how fun this is!"

I recently had the opportunity to tour Paris with a group of women for ten days. It was strange to go so far from my family and to have experiences they didn't share. Rather than give in to homesickness, I lived each moment fully for where I was and what I was doing at the time. It's a gift we each deserve to give ourselves every single day.

Albert Camus said, "Real generosity towards the future lies in giving all to the present." Yes, living in the moment is the best way to feel and practice gratitude. Why for many, and for me sometimes, is it so difficult to attain?

Jo Ann Stanley

*W*hen I was a kid, Christmas morning started with stockings. Early excitement and whispering among the children gave way to the hustle and bustle of the entire family awakening. Next came the oohs, ahs, and wows as we glimpsed the presents under the tree in the living room. But opening the stockings meant Christmas had really begun.

A candy cane hung over the felted edge of each stocking and inside were Mrs. Claus's very practical presents, cleverly disguised in bright red and green tissue paper. Despite the colorful tease, the only bona fide treats within were a sprinkling of nuts and a tangerine in the toe. My mother, whose family had suffered during the Great Depression, never seemed to appreciate the innate value of pretty or frivolous gifts. My unpretentious dad never gave a thought to shopping beyond setting a budget. Mom's sister Marge, whom we kids considered "gooney" because she wore gigantic glasses, was likewise frugal. Aunt Margie always requested useful consumables, like boxes of Kleenex. The doleful consequence of this familial parsimony was a stocking chock full of the most boring items imaginable. Every year I got a new toothbrush and maybe a tube of toothpaste. Imagine the thrill I received annually as I opened my brand new six-pack of white cotton underwear. The Christmas stockings always looked good hanging on the hearth, but when you got to the bottom you couldn't help feeling a little disappointed. This, my sixteenth year, was not yet different.

After the stockings, came coffee for my parents and breakfast for all: a special high cholesterol extravaganza of waffles or pancakes, syrup and butter, bacon or sausage, all home cooked by Mom wearing her best apron and served in our big kitchen. Then back to the living room for the important presents. Our scotch pine twinkled with colored lights and 1960's ornaments. My favorites had a space-age look to them, as if they had been purchased by the Jetsons. This particular year, four large, red, unusual envelopes nestled in the branches among the decorations, while underneath the tree laid a more typical pile of wrapped gifts.

Now that we four were older, Christmas was becoming less of a free-for-all. My little sister Mary was the youngest at age eight. Not one of us believed in Santa Claus anymore. But there was always a gift from Santa for each one of us anyway.

That year I had made candles for everyone I knew, coloring the wax with old crayons and using orange juice cans as molds. My mom must have purchased a lot of orange juice that year because I also remember using them as rollers for my hair. Anyway, I allowed myself a measure of pride over those candles as they were opened, for they had turned out much better than most of my craft experiments. I received my usual quota of gifts in return. The exchange was all very nice and civilized. In short order it seemed that except for church and dinner, Christmas was already over.

But then Mom made a speech and passed out the four envelopes, one for every kid. "I wanted each of you to have something from your grandparents," said my mom, eyes brimming over with tears. Her father had died of an aneurysm twelve years earlier. More recently, just a few months before Christmas, Mom's mother died of pancreatic cancer. Grandma had been a constant fixture in our lives, and we all missed her. Every Sunday of my childhood we went to visit Grandma in her apartment with the formal blue velvet sofa and the tray of African violets on the windowsill. She was an accomplished seamstress who made adorable outfits for my Barbie dolls out of scraps from her own dress fabrics. Normally she would be having Christmas with us.

We opened our envelopes and were completely shocked. Our parents had given each of us one thousand dollars! It was like winning the lottery. We whooped, hollered, and danced. At the time, the sum was beyond my wildest dreams. I had been working after school at my first job that year at minimum wage, $1.60 an hour. So I knew the value of a dollar—far greater than than it is now. The thought of $4,000 all in one room was astounding.

That $1,000 times four—that sum brings home to me the essential generosity of my parents. I'm sure there were many items they could have spent that money on, but they chose to give it directly to us, so that we might spend it as we wished. My parents had always seemed so tightfisted—my dad hated to spend an extra dime and my mom came from a family where nothing was ever wasted. Day to day, both were thrifty to a fault. We actually saved butter wrappers and used jelly jars for drinking glasses. But in the big picture, they gave us kids everything we ever really needed and more.

My mom spent most of that Christmas day in tears, as we all remembered stories of Grandma and Grandpa. Aunt Margie came over for dinner as she always did, bringing her ubiquitous casserole of green beans and mushroom soup topped with teeny-tiny but deliciously crispy French onion rings. After Marge had gushed over her gifts, Kleenex of course, one of those homemade candles, and a big jar of pecan halves, she and mom started all over again with the tears and the stories.

Somehow, when I recall all my Christmases, that one remains the most memorable. I can't fathom now what I spent that money on. As my father's daughter, I probably put it in the bank for college. Instead, what I remember best about that special Christmas are the tears and the love mingled so beautifully in my mother's face.

Conflict

Where the Rubber Meets the Road

People change and forget to tell each other.

—Lillian Hellman

Patricia Antonopoulos

Revolving doors are neither here nor there. They spin with the wind of push vs. shove, yet they are securely anchored to a solid center.

And that seems to be the way I approach conflict. The center of a conflict may be a value issue—a sure and certain core belief. Yet the peripherals have the power to checkmate my response.

Conflict is interactive. It requires opposing ideas. Conflict is underlined by a degree of control—of ideas, values, situations, people.

If I were to do the therapist thing and analyze why I go from shouting on stilts to whispering from a hole, it would no doubt stem from the childhood teaching that my opinions/beliefs had no value in decisions or discussions. But I am a long way from that childhood and that reasoning is weak.

Each conflict in my life is measured by the intimacy of the people surrounding the issue. There are times when I believe that the potential hurt to others might outweigh my need to address the conflict head-on. These are often the times I create intense personal conflict.

A desk clerk refusing to produce a bill for our recent stay in a motel may as well pitch a tent if he assumes I will give up and walk away without that piece of paper. I will not. I will speak softly, be polite and persist as long as it takes to resolve that conflict.

There is no emotional investment in this situation.

My adult children share their problems to the degree that they need a listening ear, a sympathetic friend, a money rescue, or other direct deposit to their well being. They know that my response is rarely critical, always polite, usually gently spoken. This conflict of values is often overwhelming, but the power lies in the relationship. My children are adults, they know what I believe, and I have no power over their decisions.

When our Thursday gatherings began, I believed we had a mutual purpose, sharing strength and courage in the absolute privacy of the group. The goal was to produce a book that would share that strength and courage with many other women.

A sense of conflict surrounded the differing ideas as to how the goals would be achieved. Adherence to attendance, to an unfailing promise that whatever was said in the meeting stayed in the meeting, start/stop times, to writing on topic, to finding the way to best meet each woman's current need, to the depth of personal sharing, to talking vs. reading our writings, all issues of some disagreement.

When I wrote and shared my life story, I opened many secret places, exposing very personal memories. In contrast, when I originally wrote about friendship, Webster could have hired me for dictionary drudge work. Later, I was asked what happened between those two pieces?

Conflict resolution happened—or at least I think it did. I pulled back in sharing my heart in favor of keeping the friendships at an easy place—avoiding conflict that might result in someone feeling the need to leave the group.

With a desk clerk, I am unemotional and determined to reach a resolution. With my children, the conflict might rage within me, but does not display. With our Cedar Roe group, I knew that resolution would evolve because we shared the same basic goal of sharing strength and courage through sharing and writing.

The entryway to my conflict resolution changes like that revolving door, moving to accommodate the value of relationships, yet anchored to that very fixed center point, a solid core in my life.

Patti Dickinson

andling conflict. Oh, boy. Conflict is everywhere. Conflict seems to increase exponentially with the number of children. More kids in more activities, rubbing elbows with others. Maybe it's a natural by-product of being a late forty-something, that seems to carry with it a certain recklessness. Calling it like I see it. Willing to swallow less. Be honest more. It is our radar. It alerts us that boundaries have been violated, that principles are at odds, that someone isn't being heard, that there is a major kink in the lines of communication. Conflict with my kids. Feeling conflicted. Feeling incensed by things I witness. In the newspaper, at school, in meetings. With my teenagers. I feel as though those of us who have clear-cut standards, standards that we established a long time ago and we've pretty much stuck by them, have a hard row to hoe.

Two kinds of conflict. The face-to-face sort of stuff, and the internal sort of discomfort that pulls at us to right a wrong, to go to bat, to fix it.

A first grade Brownie meeting. Working on the "Wave the Flag". Try-it. Talking about respect for the flag. Two girls have baseball caps on backwards, smirking throughout the discussion. I ask them to take their caps off. They glance at each other, stopping short of eye-rolling, but just barely. Outside for the flag raising. They sneak the caps under their sweatshirts to get them outside. Back on, during the flag ceremony. In your face, nothing-but-attitude. These girls are seven. Margaret is spending five days a week with these kids. Eight hours a day. This is the culture that Margaret lives in. Conflict.

Conflict with teenagers. What they wear, watch, listen to, read. What time they come home. This job demands so much more vigilance than I EVER anticipated. The wrong messages everywhere. Magazines, movies, music, peers.

Conflict. The stuff that makes me bolt awake at night. Foster kids. We live in a society that is okay with kids aging out of the foster care system. We live in a society that is okay with condoms being handed out in the high school. We live in a society that has fuzzy, wavy lines concerning what's right, what's wrong. We live in a society where too many parents don't know how to say no to a kid that is over the age of twelve. We live in a society that thinks that "Just say no" can fix it right up. We live in a society that says safe sex is a nice compromise. Instead of standing our ground, we've lowered the bar. The majority of us say nothing when over-functioning parents bully kids on soccer and baseball fields and basketball courts. Sportsmanship is given lip service. Where our children's social skills are faltering because parents won't get out of the way and let children resolve their own conflict. Where parents tell kids when to swing, when to run to the next base, whom to throw the ball to. Who brings oranges. Who brings pop. Who stays on the team; who needs a team that is not quite as competitive. Where nice no longer matters. We live in a society that has had its President a little fuzzy on the definition of sex. And we call this man our leader. I am conflicted about the lack of dignity. That we can advertise Viagra on prime-time television. That there is no subject too delicate to talk about on the radio, see on television or on the big screen. That we are willing to let Hollywood feed us a steady diet of filth and call it entertainment. Yes, conflicted. Outraged. Saddened. Wishing that my children could enjoy the same sort of childhood that I can reminisce about. Roaming the neighborhood. Where the village took its job seriously. Where parents drew the line in the sand. A time where kids were more secure because they knew someone was in charge. When parents were parents and not trying to be their kids' friend.

The interpersonal, face-to-face stuff is more difficult. In marriage, Wood and I have had to learn how to settle our differences in a sort of verbal Cliff Notes. Decisions get made often without the due-diligence conversation because of a time crunch or just being weary to the bone. This sometimes leads to stuff that isn't completely resolved resurfacing later. We have learned to choose our battles.

I shy away from conflict, instinctually. Seldom initiate a confrontation with adults outside my family. I just sort of back away and get a little distance. I like to deal with conflict calmly, quietly with no one raising his or her voice.

I think that how we deal with conflict probably has an awful lot to say about how we view ourselves. Conflict at its worst is about being right. Conflict at its best is about finding a place to begin. Not about compromise. Maybe it's all about being heard. Listening with the heart, not the head.

Shawna Samuel

I would rather eat a box of nails than have a conflict with someone. I am a peacemaker, an unsolicited emotional barometer for all who surround me. I can pick up on a subtlety that indicates conflict is coming, and I want to turn and run. But I don't. I stay, and I generally try to make it all right. As I've aged I've become more able to deal with conflict and meet it head-on. At least I have learned how to face it without it disabling me.

I have a friend who is so able and calm when it comes to conflict. She doesn't get ruffled or emotional; instead, she manages to get right at the heart of the issue to pursue a peaceful solution. I strive to be that way. In fact, I've learned that conflict is much easier to resolve if I can just dive right in and face it.

Of course, conflicts have different faces, and each carries its own wrinkles. Conflicts with children are to be expected, and with the role of parent clearly defined, I can rise to those conflicts more easily. The personal conflicts that hit close to home are the most difficult. It is when my emotions get involved that I get into trouble. A conflict with my mother, husband or a friend is the toughest of all. In avoiding conflicts with the people I love, I don't face issues that have hurt or angered me. So when I do finally get to the point of addressing a conflict, I'm usually so angry and emotional that I go totally overboard. Without anger pushing me on, it's hard for me to say things that are unpleasant or hurtful, even when I know it will clear the air. I think I always want to be fair and measured, but sometimes thoughts and feelings are anything but. Sometimes they are unjust, ugly and harsh.

As I age, business-related conflicts become easier to handle. I have a job in government, and have seen politics at their best and worst. Honesty, openness, and learning that sometimes when you most want to say something it is most important to say nothing, have helped me in this endeavor. I've also learned not to take professional situations personally, and I'm accepting more easily the fact that I cannot do things perfectly. And neither does anyone else.

Hopefully, as I get older, that box of nails won't be so appealing.

Jo Ann Stanley

I know it's just a phase, akin to the terrible twos, when the child seeks greater autonomy and independence, asserting the self as separate from the parent. But when they were two, they were little and cute. If one of them stamped a foot, folded arms across the chest, or turned down the mouth in a pout, it was tempting to laugh; it was necessary to hide a smile behind my hand as I attempted to take a serious tone. Then, they were just so adorable, with big blue eyes and curly mops. Now, they're more or less at their worst, either gangly or pudgy with braces and acne. Now, when one stamps a foot it's not funny at all, because that's usually the prelude to a zinging insult and a slammed bedroom door. All parents experience the conflict I'm writing about: it's us versus them, the adolescents.

Case in point: daughter number one, age fifteen and very moody. A great student, she works hard all week at school, so on weekends she sleeps until noon, then roams the house all night. At three in the morning my husband and I jolt awake at the sound of the blender because she's in the kitchen making a banana peach smoothie. Will the dishes be washed by morning? Certainly not. Instead, gross orange-brown leftover smoothie still oozes from the blender in the sink while the forgotten glass etches a ring in the coffee table. Last Saturday at 2:00 in the afternoon, she was on the back patio lying in the sun, still wearing her purple plaid pj's, hair uncombed, bed not made, chores not done, six hours of homework ignored and forgotten. But if I say anything at all about responsibilities, even a gentle suggestion or hint that the day is slipping away, she bites back that I'm an intolerable nag.

Daughter number two: age fourteen and very social. Our major issues: skimpy clothes, too much make-up, constant and irritating phone calls, household rules. One of her jean skirts was so tight that I had to slip it into the charity bag while she was at school. During dinner and flute practice my husband takes the phone off the hook. Not only that, we're so unreasonable that we won't get her own line or purchase her a cell phone. More than once she's been sent to her bedroom to change before leaving the house, but just as often she's given us the slip and gotten out of here with an objectionable outfit, like shorts with words on the bottom. My major fears: sex, drugs, alcohol and peer pressure; vulnerability, safety, senseless risks and sex offenders. She tells me my fears are ridiculous, and generally, it's true that she's a responsible, sensible child. Yet lately, she's been testing the limits. When I lay down the law, or simply say no, I'm accused of being an unreasonable, judgmental hag.

So here you have the crux of my conflict—which is it?—Am I hag or nag? Oh my gosh, I'm both. How horrible. What have they done to me, what have I done to myself? How can I allow their constant pushing and chafing to corner me to the point that I'm capable of acting like someone I wouldn't even want to know? It's entrapment!

At age two, the worst they could say was "No!" Then I'd scoop them up and tickle their tummies. Now they're like seasoned lawyers, with catchy arguments, slick phrases, smarmy ridicule and taut sarcasm. I'm generally not allowed to touch them, hug them, or kiss them, and the worst they can say is—well, I can't bring myself to say it.

CHANCE ENCOUNTERS

Wisdom Through Strangers

One can never pay in gratitude; one can only pay "in kind" somewhere else in life.

—Anne Morrow Lindbergh

Patricia Antonopoulos

Four times the stranger stood close to an opportunity.
Four times the stranger understood the need.
Four times the stranger felt with compassion.
Four times the stranger failed to make a difference.

Three younger children were being watched by a boy about ten years old, a baby in the cart seat and two other children hanging onto the sides. As the cart started to tip, the boy struggled to keep it upright, jarring his glasses and ball cap. Reaching out to help steady the cart, I told the boy what a great big brother he was, how strong he was, that his mother must be very proud of him.

At the sound of the struggle, the mother stepped from behind a display, her angry face scarlet. Through clenched teeth, she hissed her command that the children behave or else. The ten-year-old boy wilted, head down, face contorted.

Two children were grabbing item after item whining repeated requests at Dad. Dad's "shut up and put the (expletive) back!" had little effect. Making faces behind his back, the children smirked at one another and continued. Suddenly, Dad grabbed the latest items from their hands, threw the candy into the cart, and hit the closest child. "I'll buy the (expletive) things if you shut your ugly faces." The kids shared a victory smirk.

A mother, with a baby in the cart, was shouting at a daughter eight or nine years old. Their disagreement was over the style of shorts to purchase. The mother spoke with contempt of the girl's choice of simple dark unisex shorts. "Until you dress like a girl and not some damn homo, you aren't getting anything new."

An obese woman, mid-fifties, using a cane, came into the doctors' building with a waif of a child—a girl about 11 or 12. The girl struggled with a huge backpack and an armload of books. As they sat next to me, I commented on what must be an overload of homework.

The girl answered without moving her lips and I had no idea what she said. The woman glared. Ignoring me, she directed her anger to the girl. "I don't want to hear your problems. Put the stuff in your backpack and shut up!"

As the girl fought to force more into the bag, the woman got up and walked away. Panicked, the child jumped up and asked where her mother was going. "Bathroom. Stay."

"I hate it when she walks away from me. She says she will leave me all alone. I was born at the other St. Luke's. Do you like this St. Luke's? Is this St. Luke's? Doesn't look like it? Is my mother coming back?" Exploding speech.

Time for a deep breath.

As I helped rearrange the backpack, I struggled for a voice of comfort. "Of course your mother will be back. If she loses her way, we will go find her. The other St. Luke's had a happy day when you were born there, but this isn't St. Luke's. The next building to the left is St. Luke's Hospital."

"She will kill me now!"

A man coming in from the parking lot spoke to the girl. "Where is she?"

"In the bathroom, but Daddy this lady said we are in the wrong place. This isn't St. Luke's." "Shut up," was the response to this agitated, disheveled child.

This little girl, this child, did not register any surprise at his words. She just stood up and wandered away, a kind of hopelessness etched on every part of her.

Four times, the stranger was there—there in a place of need.
Four times, the stranger had some wisdom rooted in compassion.
Four times the stranger failed to make a difference.
I was the stranger.

Patti Dickinson

*E*arly this fall, one of my most favorite kids made the newspaper. Her smiling face, huddled second from the left in the black and white photo, among three other faces that would be the freshmen class officers at Shawnee Mission East for 2002-2003. Joy redefined on her eager face. I imagine some major button-popping episodes going on with the mom and dad whom I just happen to like a whole lot, too.

So I put the paper on top of the microwave where everything of importance sits in a holding pattern for some length of time before action is taken. Thought about having one of the kids run it down to Stark's, as I'd sent Andrew over to Brake's with Jen's tennis accomplishments in print many times over the last four years. Newspapers record history.

Decided to frame the newspaper clipping. That way, it wouldn't wind up under her bed, or stuffed in a drawer, or yellowed. It would be preserved. This was history, after all. To the Fairway Frame Shop. Push open that heavy glass door that sticks and the bell that hangs from the wall directly over the door announces my presence. I've known these people for a long time. They've framed just about every kid-manufactured work of art in my house. (Now that I think about it, that might be about ALL I've got hanging in my house!)

I told them right off that I needed Shawnee Mission East's colors for the mat. My three teenagers assured me that that was the way to go. Black was not a problem. The blue was. Two other customers in the shop, two employees and myself. All had an opinion. Eventually we had a consensus. I stood back. What did I know, I had kids at Bishop Miege. Red and blue. An easily identifiable blue.

One of the customers left. The other stayed. She said, "That is such a nice thing you are doing for your young friend." And I said with a wave of my hand, "Oh it has sat on the microwave—finally getting around to doing something with it. . ." and she put both her hands on my forearms, as she pulled herself

151

toward me and looked into my eyes, creating a feeling of intimacy where there really shouldn't be any. I'd just gotten a little advice about the shade of blue, after all. She said, "I would guess that several people thought about doing what you did. But you acted on the thought. That made all the difference; don't you see?" And with that, she smiled a kind and gentle smile. And jangled the bells as she opened that heavy glass door. Her words hung in the air.

As the seconds ticked, the bells continued to jangle against the door, a little softer each time they hit. I could still feel the imprint of the stranger's fingers on my arms. I could think of nothing but the words that are said at Sunday Mass, in the penitential rite, asking forgiveness for what we have done, and what we have failed to do. I have spoken those words since I was a little girl, but here was a light bulb moment. For it was in the doing that I realized how many times I had failed to do. Had the opportunity and didn't do. Meant to but. . . wanted to but. . . tried to but. . . could have, but didn't. Opportunities to make a difference that fell by the wayside. How many times had some small, seemingly insignificant thing such as this been crowded out of the schedule because ordinary things crowded in? Too tired. Too busy. Too just-about-anything. And that intention fell into that horrible category of nice-but-not-necessary.

Optional.

Maybe nice isn't optional, after all.

Shawna Samuel

There was one day that a meeting with a stranger changed the course of my life. I was 16 years old and looking for an office job, one that I could attend after school and during the summer. I had pounded the pavement for weeks when I went into Old American Insurance Company. I filled out my application, turned it into the receptionist and was leaving when, as an afterthought, she called after me. I almost didn't hear her and walked on. She said, "You know, it's a fluke, but you might try upstairs. There's a small banking consultant firm that rents space from us. It's only an office of four, but they might need some help." Why not, I thought.

So I went upstairs, and coming out into the hallway was Sue Bray.

"Hi," she said with her warm, friendly smile.

I worked by her side for five years and learned so much. She is now one of my closest friends. I'd worked there for two years when I met my husband, Duncan. Sue met her husband, Garry, around the same time. They are now the godparents of our children. They are two of the finest, most wonderful people we've ever known. Duncan and I feel honored to have them in our lives.

To think if I hadn't heard the receptionist and turned back.

Jo Ann Stanley

*H*ow could he know so much about me? He was a stranger, after all. We were waiting for the bus to arrive, in a dusty town in southern Colombia. We waited over five hours. So we had plenty of time to kill.

He didn't really look like a gypsy—more like a bum, in fact. But he had the dark hair and swarthy complexion one expects of a gypsy. He was probably forty-five years old. His black felt hat was no fedora. His scarlet neckerchief was certainly silk, but raggedy and frayed. I confess I was a little startled when he first came up to me. Gypsy meets gringa.

"*Dame tu mano*—give me your hand," he implored. Why not? So I held out my hand, which he took in both of his greasy ones. With his index finger he traced the lines, more than once. I was ready to withdraw it when he started speaking. I knew enough Spanish to follow most of what he said.

"You're at a crossroads—" he began. (No brainer. This town wasn't much else.) I wasn't exactly impressed. But then he went on. Here's the gist:

"There are two loves in your life" he knew, "and you can't decide between them. One is all heart. The other you can't be sure of, not yet. See here—where your love line forks? Here you stand, unable to decide. Should you go back to one of them? Which one? Should you go back at all?

"But you're on your way back. So go on. Go back and leave the one that loves you, pursue the one you love. I can tell you're depressed about this. But it's only your period."

That shocked me for sure. How did this gypsy guy know I was on the rag? That was embarrassing to think about. And how could he know so much about my love life? How had he read my mind? But he was right. I had that very day been worrying about my homecoming. I did have to make those decisions. It was true. I had menstrual cramps and menstrual blues. He was right about everything.

I'll never forget my gypsy fortuneteller. It was more than a dozen years before it all played out. But I left the one who loved me, and married the one I loved.

SEPTEMBER 11, 2001

One Year Later

The ultimate measure of a man is not where he stands
in moments of comfort and convenience,
but where he stands in times of challenge and controversy.

—Martin Luther King

Patricia Antonopoulos

Perspective is not possible. Understanding and balance are too far from our reach.

If our great grandchildren truly remember, perhaps they will have a perspective, a balance, an understanding of September 11, 2001.

Unless we have been students of international politics and historical perspectives, we cannot begin to understand the current position of the United States in world interaction.

On the anniversaries of September 11, I will not turn on the television nor listen to the radio. Seeing the towers fall again and reliving the stories of heroism will pour acid on a raw sore.

September 11 will eventually become the Crusades, Antietam, the Holocaust, Biafra, Kosovo, Hungary, apartheid, and slavery—all the obscene and devastating paragraphs in the study of man—raw and aching places impossible to heal.

September 11 is a new center point in an immense series of connections displaying both the majesty and the darkness of humans.

We have been swept into currents unknown before that date. Heroism has been revisited, unfailingly defined. Evil has new synonyms.

Generosity and greed have found Ground Zero, and joined in a fresh alliance.

What I believe about September 11, is just beyond my intellectual and emotional reach. It is a haunt that will not move into a place where I can safely store that memory.

Patti Dickinson

I got up this morning, having made the decision that I wasn't going to listen to the radio or watch television. I wanted to hear no platitudes, no trite media spins, no "Good Morning America" interviews, no sound bites, no shallow rehash of what had already been said. Nothing that would disturb the sanctity and dignity of the day. Wood lowered the flag to half-mast, and we took Andrew to meet the bus that left that morning for two nights and three days of team-building at Wildwood, a long-standing traditional field trip for sixth graders.

I spent the day very aware of how I was choosing to spend my time. What I did with the day was no different than any other day—a little laundry, a quick run to Indian Hills to bring Mary Morgan an Advil to get rid of her headache. A tuna fish sandwich on rye bread for lunch. I sat in the sunshine at Westwood View with a friend, as she showed me how to shape the neck of a pumpkin sweater I was knitting. Or trying to. So although the rhythm of the day remained the same, the background music, my thoughts, were ones of gratitude and contentment for the everyday sameness of my life.

Yet there was also an intrusive sense of grief. My two youngest girls now know and can use correctly in a sentence, "terrorist."

Shawna Samuel

How do you get your mind around such an event as 9/11, much less your heart and soul? What can I do? What is my part? How can I help? I am overwhelmed by the largeness of the problems in the Middle East. By comparison, my life is so small, so protected, not at all a part of the whole.

As for all Americans fortunate to grow up in a free society, full of opportunities, terrorism finds no understanding in my mind. For better or for worse, I cannot tackle the larger issues. For no matter how I try to find an answer, I always come back to my personal solution: living the best life that I can. I'm not talking about lifestyle; I'm talking about living life as a good person. For me it means taking personal responsibility, from little things to big; doing the right thing, even when nobody's watching, especially when nobody's watching. It means living as a person of honor, who respects other people, who does what she says she'll do, who is honest and fair, and who gives her time to the community, family and friends. It means raising responsible children who don't just think of themselves, and who are grateful they were born in America. To me, the little things you can choose to do in life add up to the important big picture.

The news coverage of 9/11 makes me question the priorities in this society. Why must we all drag ourselves over and over through our horrible tragedies? I feel that I'm invading someone's privacy to witness their tears over their loss of a loved one. Am I alone? Apparently I am, judging by the daily news shows and special reports. It seems that the more horrific the event, the more minutes are spent covering it.

I do not watch it; I cannot watch it, for with each passing second I feel smaller, more insignificant, and more helpless and overwhelmed. But just imagine, if only for a moment, what the world would be like if everyone lived their lives with honesty, integrity, kindness, and with a steady moral compass. Imagine if every single person respected others, their choices and their freedom. Imagine the peace and happiness in our world, our nation, and our neighborhoods. Imagine.

Then, I don't feel like what I'm doing is really so small after all.

Jo Ann Stanley

For me, like so many, September 11, 2001 began with blue skies and gorgeous weather. In Kansas City as in New York, that day of horror began innocently. I dropped the kids at school and got busy with routine chores and errands.

I was in the checkout line at the grocery store when I overheard a few phrases about the attack without really understanding what was happening: "plane," "World Trade Center," "New York." I came home and turned on the TV just in time to see the first building crumble live. Tears streamed down my face as the groceries warmed on the kitchen counter. I sank into the sofa in confusion and despair and stared at the TV.

Like so many, I spent the day glued to the television watching events unfold. As more information became available I began to worry about loved ones: my husband who had plans to go out of town on business (his flight was cancelled); my brother and his wife in Washington, D.C.; all my friends who live and work in D.C., which is my hometown; my in-laws in Pennsylvania; and my friends in New York, especially my college buddy, Andy.

I was particularly concerned about my friend Andy, a lawyer, because I knew he worked near the World Trade Center. Before the tragedy, his building was on the block facing the twin towers. As the news worsened and I watched pictures of people wandering the streets of New York covered in dust, I tried to call Andy, but of course phone lines were jammed. I ended up leaving a message of concern on his home phone in Rye. The next day I heard he was okay. On September 13, I received Andy's email and read details of his story.

On his way to work that morning, Andy emerged from the subway shortly after 9:00 a.m. and found crowds of people pointing at the World Trade Center, exclaiming about the plane that had run into the building when suddenly they all saw a second plane hit the other tower. Andy, like everyone else, was in shock but no one felt any imminent danger—all their concern was for the people who were actually in the towers. As in a ticker tape parade, bits of office paper floated down to the streets. He was standing in a group of people who were reacting to what was happening, wondering how to help and also how to explain it, when the first tower disintegrated. Instantly all was nuclear winter and chaos. Andy never saw the people he had been talking with again that day and only heard later that each had survived with a completely different story than his own. Choking and showered with dust, Andy stumbled into a doorway where several strangers huddled. Someone handed him a bottle of water and he gulped it down. Realizing he wasn't injured, Andy wandered out in a daze. Paper and debris swirled in the streets. He started walking without any destination; his only thought was to keep walking, away from screaming, death and dust. In times of war, his state of being would termed "shell-shocked." But this wasn't a war, or if it was, he didn't know it yet. Eventually he thought of his cell phone and tried to call his wife, so that Marcia would know that he was okay. The cell wasn't working. As he walked further from the blast and people recognized that he had come from the disaster, he was greeted again and again and asked if he needed help. He was given water and food and offered sanctuary. He was eventually able to telephone Marcia from someone's office.

Andy says he was never prouder to be a New Yorker than on that day, when every single person in that city was moved to help one another in any way possible. As he walked along Andy realized that he only wanted to go home, to hold his wife in his arms and to embrace his three daughters. As the rumors and bits of news reached him, he began to have some sense of how lucky he was to be alive. He heard that the second tower also fell. He walked over four miles to the train station to take the train out of the city and home to Rye, New York, about an hour's journey by rail. His eyes burned, his throat was clogged, but he was okay.

Andy wasn't able to return to his office for months, as it was next door to ground zero. He had been wearing a favorite tie that day and was sure it was ruined, but he took it to the cleaner's anyway, and they restored it, beautifully, and wouldn't charge a dime. Now he never wears that tie; it hangs in his closet as a reminder.

An interesting irony in Andy's story is that as a criminal lawyer he actually defended one of those accused in the first World Trade Center bombings. He explains that his guy actually had nothing to do with it, but was of the "wrong" ethnic origin and his voice was caught on a tape with one of the other conspirators. Andy believes passionately in the American justice system and that everyone, guilty or not, has a right to a fair trial. That's why he became a criminal lawyer. He's had some real scum bags for clients, drug dealers and now this bomb suspect.

I don't envy Andy his job. Especially now, after 9/11. Yet I am glad that there are lawyers like Andy devoted to human rights, even in the face of the most despicable terrorism. Those inalienable rights are part of what makes America a great country; it's because we're a great and powerful country that we have become the target of terrorists. Compromising our democratic system will never eradicate terrorism; it will only mean that we've lost one of our strengths.

Andy's a big man, burly, a giant teddy bear who painted rainbow murals on his daughters' bedroom wall.

Yes, I'm glad Andy's alive today.

BUT NOT FOR MEDIOCRITY

Learning

The problems we experience are not so much to do with who we are
as to holding back who we really are.

—Albert Einstein

Patricia Antonopoulos

Not personally crafted words meaningful to the wedding couple, but time-tested vows spoken to the understanding of generations . . .for better and for worse.

When we reflect, the worse usually looks like those things we fear most, abject poverty, crushing illness, mental deterioration, death, seemingly unbearable loss. Love, fresh, new and passionate covers all the imagined with a down comforter. Together we can grow richer in our love as we handle the worse, whatever that might be.

The truth is that mediocrity is the ruler of that vow to accept the worse. Dreadful things, the harshness of life, will put our hands together, holding one another's needs with all the delicacy we own. Often, the tragedies can be the events most likely to test and prove our commitment. We learn to cherish as we learn to struggle.

So we have better and worse as the touchstone of marriage, the highs and the lows that are suppose to be our joys/sorrows, victories/defeats, life/death kinds of passages. But the fulcrum is the piece that holds the balancing act of for better and for worse. And the fulcrum is mediocrity.

It is so hard to go through the days and nights of sugarless vanilla pudding, the times of bland. Sloshing through, dragging from one chore to the next, sometimes longing for even an argument to stop this slow cancer on a marriage. These are the times when we know, without any doubt, that mediocrity is the true bottom feeder, eating away at both the joy of better and the strength of worse.

Often, during times of distancing, we close off; shutdown and insulate from the person we love most, the person who should be getting the energies we are using for all of the others who seem to appreciate us more. Our need is to give, but not to someone who takes the giving for granted. The ebb of passion needs replacement and mediocrity is not the aphrodisiac of choice.

From my side of the bed the look and feel is only mine . . . three emaciated feather pillows in laundry softened cases, a down comforter across the foot, colorless terry robe slung on the bed post, piles of books, crossword puzzles, pencils and a couple of Tylenol on the table.

If it were possible to starch half a sheet...the perfect solution. He needs military precision, sheets tightened to bounce that quarter, one large, unyielding foam pillow in our best white (and ironed) case, robe huge neatly, and no bedside table required. Yet I require that military neatness in the most of the house and he never, ever sees dust.

A sense of the ocean fits my need to make it through each period of mediocrity. Times of power and passion, of storms, leave the beach scattered with the leavings of day to day. A gentle cleansing tide allows the moldy scrim, the mediocrity, to drift away. And the vow is relived yet another time.

Patti Dickinson

We have been married for thirty years. We met when I was fifteen, he sixteen. We were together six years before we married, so we have known each other for more than two-thirds of our lives. And I think that I am still learning about this spouse of mine . . .where it hurts and why, what's funny, how we function or don't in a crisis, what brings tears, what scares us.

Marriage is such an interesting lifestyle. Two people, purportedly adults, commit to "until death do us part." To me, it is miraculous when it works.

Marriage is an institution that is intensely personal. Not like child rearing, which is so closely tied-in with that village concept. Everyone's got an opinion on discipline, when to stop breast feeding, teenage curfews. But uncapped toothpaste tubes, infidelity, cell phones interrupting dinner, how much to spend/save, who mows. Dangerous waters. Marriage—no one really knows what goes on in other people's marriages. We get our information on frequency of sex from Good Housekeeping's poll. And even more amazing, we read that stuff; we use that information as a yardstick for where on the continuum we fall. (Just as an aside—what if everyone they polled LIED?)

Mostly, we laugh about the things that are irritating. Standing over the suitcases, the night before we leave on a trip...almost a work of art, what I have accomplished. Packing suitcases for ten of us to travel halfway across the country. All the things that have to be remembered. The Dramamine, the contact lens solution. the allergy medicine, batteries for the CD players (double A), nail clippers. Packed so that ten individuals can recreate all the comforts of home, while away. I am NOT open to ANY suggestions. Compliments on peak efficiency, YES. Better ways to reorganize. Not a chance. And so I laugh, or try to. And my husband continues to give me unwanted advice. To the point that when he adjusts one more shoe in the suitcase I am gnashing my molars together.

Not all silences are bad.

We don't talk about marriages that have gone off-track because it is a reflection on ourselves. Infidelity. It would take an incredible self-esteem to be able to talk about your spouse's transgression.

To be honest, I am not sure that our marriage has been characterized by much mediocrity. The everyday, the routine, certainly. But mediocrity has a ring of indifference. A shade-of-gray mentality. And I work hard, maybe too hard to combat that. Confrontation is very difficult for me, but not in marriage. I want the problem ON THE TABLE. Out into the light of day where it can't fester. Out there where we both can see it, feel it, taste it. And it is there for BOTH of us to work on.

We come to marriage with a lot of how-it's-done having been modeled for us. We didn't come with much. Oh, we came with lots of stuff that we knew should just be thrown in the trash...and we have had to learn how to be the couple we wanted to be. It meant not living out of the past. It meant that the language of disagreement needed to be tempered with gentleness. It meant that affection needed to be learned. It meant that apologies needed to be expressed. Not in an off-handed way, not tossed over your shoulder as you're leaving the room. But a face-to-face, look-me-in-the-eyes-and-you'd-better-look-sincere kind of an apology.

Maybe the ebb and flow of our marriage has been characterized by moments where we were content, where life together was the union of two people who each knew who they were in relation to each other. We have had some moments of deep despair—several miscarriages, a runaway kid. Those moments have been characterized by pulling inward, away. That retreat that felt so awful at the time, gave us the power to heal, to reunite in better psychological shape. And there have been moments—the birth of a baby, a success of a kid. Those milestone things, where you can grasp the overwhelmed feeling of a joint success.

No mediocrity in this marriage. And the day-to-day, spent with someone who really does know how to separate the wheat from the chaff—a place where I can be, just be. Where I can grow old gracefully and wear my lumps and wrinkles as a badge of a life well-lived without worrying that someone better will come along, is the best part of marriage. Maybe it defines contentment.

Shawna Samuel

I rise from my bed, having to dislodge a peaceful cat who is curled up behind my knees, to write this. I've given a lot of thought to this particular writing assignment, but cannot seem to make myself sit down and write it. For better or for worse, but not for mediocre. This assignment has made me dwell upon what, exactly, mediocre is.

We've had a busy day, no big surprise. Finally sat down about nine o'clock. Watched one TV show, and we turned it off and went up to bed. Brushed teeth, checked on the kids, filled the cats' crunchy bowl.

Oh, I thought. This is mediocre!

I live my life largely guided by what's right and wrong. If it's right, I generally do it, and if it's wrong, I generally don't. I took the wedding vows seriously. I wouldn't stray. I have and will always be faithful. I know that about Duncan as well. I married him for better or for worse. We are raising children together. I have often wondered how people could put their children through such a huge change as divorce. Isn't it just easier to stay married? Well, Duncan is such a gentle, nice person, it's easy for me to say that. Unfortunately, many women are not so blessed.

Marriage, love, it's all so confusing. We bring baggage from the past, events that have shaped us. We bring expectations and dreams for the future. We respond to changes around us and in us. There is respect, dominance, appeal… so many factors that make love work. It, like so many things, is a balancing act.

When Duncan was my age, we'd been married two years. I feel like I've just blinked my eyes and bam, here we are nearly two decades later. I've now been married nearly half my life. I feel like I'm going to blink again, and bam, I'll be 61. Life is short. Life is precious. I don't expect the fireworks of the early years. I understand, accept and fully appreciate the gentle, deep, accepting love that replaces the fireworks. I respect and marvel at how that stage arrives approximately the same time the cellulite does. Works for me. But being married to someone older has made me see the wonders and ravages of time and how quickly it flies by. Is this how other women feel?

I've told Duncan in these last few weeks that I do not care about being married to a successful man. I do not care about being married to a rich man. But I do want to be married to a happy man. That for me is the opposite of mediocre.

Jo Ann Stanley

Perhaps 5,000 of us crammed together at the venue. So many were coming down the stairs that none of us could go up. A cop halted all. Eventually, we were permitted passage. We snaked our way, weaving through wall-to-wall bodies toward the stage, and actually found ourselves two seats two rows apart. We sat. We waited. We wished we had beer. We were between bands, listening to prerecorded schlock and the organizer, "Bear with us, folks." Then "they" came on. I wouldn't have minded if "they" were the Chieftains. But not all this hassle, not for mediocrity.

Another time, an evening with the girls. A classic ladies' night out. What a treat, to spend time with other women, out on the town, with *tapas* and *vino* and stimulating conversation. OOPS! What went wrong? Are they really talking about potty training? Our children are in college, for God's sake. Oh, no, someone else has an anecdote to share. Pee! Poop! Even the twenty-something can discuss her nanny gig. I can't believe it. I was looking forward to this evening, but not for mediocrity!

A final example: our president. The C student at Yale. How many dollars spent on war? How many soldiers dead in Iraq? I believe in personal sacrifice. I believe in freedom. But I don't believe in American supremacy. I am a citizen of the globe. I wish to lessen our dependence on foreign oil, not ruin the planet. Why don't we use American ingenuity rather than American clout? I didn't vote for this president. I didn't vote for mediocrity.

DEATH

Losing a Loved One

I don't want to get to the end of my life
and find that I just lived the length of it.
I want to have lived the width of it as well.
—Diane Ackerman

Patricia Antonopoulos

Throughout much of our lives, death can be an opaque presence barely noticeable in some parts of our consciousness. When we encounter the death of someone close to us, the topic becomes intimate. That death of a loved one can be a gateway to our own living, renewing our hopes and efforts. A single death can be a powerful reminder of the need to protect love, to embrace a new sense of purpose. Death can diminish failures and intensify resolve.

Innocence, joy, spontaneity, acceptance—the freedom of childhood could become the freedom of a lifetime if death were embraced rather than feared.

There is meaning to the thread that takes us from total dependence, growing independence, presumed adult/independence, and back to the dependence of the last stages of life.

Many religious people profess a belief in life after physical death. This after-life is a reward, a greater life, a perfect life. The number of professing people truly living the belief is much smaller. We cling to this physical life, not wanting to let it go.

A life well lived is the process of finding our way towards making the world more—simply more. Mrs. Rumphius, a character in a children's book, scatters lupine seeds as she walks and each spring her beauty blooms again. Adding beauty in any form to the lives around us is scattering seeds that multiply.

Death is not yet my friend, but my aging and experiencing the deaths of many loved ones takes me closer to understanding.

It is about acceptance. To accept that our life will be over at a time probably not of our choosing can bring a combination of urgency of the moment and acceptance of limitations. It appears that physical infirmity diminishes the fear and may even bring a welcoming spirit. The balance between life and death has something to do with the perceived quality of life. Life is easier to cherish when the body has not overcome the spirit.

Accepting one's own death is the process of grieving. That grieving can be focused on the loss of our life, or it can be grieving that choices have not been of the quality to allow us to embrace and celebrate our life.

Perhaps the death of a loved one is a gateway to our own living, renewing our hopes and efforts. Death can be a powerful reminder of the need to protect love, to embrace a new sense of purpose. Death can diminish our failures and intensify our resolve.

Patti Dickinson

eath. I've lost two grandmothers, a college roommate, Wood's dad, his grandmother and his brother. The dead, no pulse, bury-in-the-ground kind of death.

There are other kinds of death, though. Huge emotional losses. Matt. February 11, 2001. Flew out of KCI for Mayport, Florida and seemingly never looked back. Just—gone. Elizabeth walked out of the house December 15, 2001. Two-thousand-and-one might have been a great movie, but it was not a good year.

Sorting through what feels like rubble. Pieces of someone else's life. Matt's stuff lined up against the wall in the basement in cardboard boxes. Right before he went to boot camp, me insisting, he getting testy about cleaning up that room. Andrew poised to occupy the space that his big brother was vacating. I didn't know what Matt wanted to keep, what he wanted to save. Wasn't a job I could do. Kind of a moving-on-to-the-next-stage kind of passage. Never did get it done right. Boxes of—stuff. Stuff that was important to him. Once. Not sure what's important to him now. I've missed so much. Missed a year of him. Missed turning the corner. Miss him.

The rubble in Elizabeth's room is a different sort of rubble. Left in a hurry. Left so much. Not packaged, boxed. But left in the same sort of way that she ran her life—in a funky, gentle, quiet, make-no-waves sort of way. That's the sting—she was making waves. Artistic ripples. A rhythm was beginning. An ebb and flow. The week after she left I sat on her bed. I looked around the room. I tried to breathe in the essence of her. Tried to figure out just what made this kid of mine tick. I cleaned out dresser drawers, making piles, categories of stuff. T-shirts, long and short-sleeved. Underwear, socks. But I couldn't touch the art stuff. I couldn't "categorize" it. Felt invasive. Felt intrusive. Felt like I had no business doing that. That was hers and hers alone. What was I making room for anyway?

How they've left their stuff behind is so similar to how their personalities are. Ironic, huh? Matt, neat, orderly. Packaged, contained in his emotions. What remains of him boxed, stacked, lining the wall of the basement opposite the hot water heater. Elizabeth's art closet seemingly no order, sort of bursting at the seams, taking up a whole bunch of space. Not easily contained. An overflow sort of feeling. Only she understood the inherent order of this chaos.

I wonder why these two kids of mine can so easily walk away. From their things, from trinkets that once had value, that connect them to the memories. Memories that represent the moments of their lives. "Life provides only a few moments. For these moments we live our lives." Words of a young seminarian on a senior year retreat in high school. Powerful words. All these years later. Those moments that helped shape them into who they are, perhaps maybe who they can become. From connections that seemingly have no more meaning to them. Amidst all this rubble, it feels like no life can emerge. Feels like unfinished business.

Shawna Samuel

I said my final goodbye to my grandmother Veta last week. Alzheimer's is a twisted, tortured illness that forces loved ones to say goodbye over and over again. This journey has taken nearly five years. At first, she just repeated things in the same conversation. Then she couldn't find the words she was looking for, then she became paranoid and hallucinated. There were many difficult stages, but it was far more difficult to move her out of her home than it was to let her go be with God; to be free of her body and tortured mind.

When we first moved her from her home, she was fidgety and nervous. She got out her wallet in the car, moved everything around, and would play with things, hide things, lose things. In fact, she lost her wedding ring, a distinctive ring I had seen on her hand for all of my 40 years. Veta had wonderful hands. I can still see her rubbing a cat's ears, working in the dirt to plant a flower, or washing dishes. She massaged the dishes in lukewarm water and lemon soap, a soap I use today because it reminds me of her.

There were many painful steps along this journey, but I am grateful, so very grateful that she never stopped knowing my family and me. She may not have been able to name us, but she always recognized us as her favorite people, her family. She called me her baby for the last few years.

The last visit I had with her was before I left on a weekend trip with my college girlfriends. It was a wonderful visit. I fed her lunch, and she ate well. I could be as slow and patient as she needed because she was the center of my attention, not one of many to feed like the aides had. She enjoyed that slow pace. I made her custard, without nutmeg, which she seemed to enjoy. When I left for home, I cradled her face in my hands and told her I loved her, and kissed her. She clearly said "I love you too" and gave me a whiskery, toothless kiss. They were wheeling her down the hall as I turned to leave.

The very night I returned home from my trip, I got a late-night call from her nurse saying that she was struggling for air, her respiration was over 50 breaths per minute, and her pulse was thready. She was so agitated, could they give her morphine, knowing that that might enable her to slip away?

Yes, of course, I said. But, I asked, this doesn't mean we have to keep her on morphine, right? She can come back, right? Yes, she could, was the answer I got. How naive I was. You would think that with all these years to prepare, I would be ready. I wasn't. I went to see her early the next morning, and spent all day holding her hand. She was in a coma, seemed comfortable, relaxed and warm. They had some nice music playing for her. The doctor came in and examined her and said that she probably didn't have more than 24 hours left. I called all the family, and my church. I polished her fingernails and put lotion on her hands, something I did almost every week. Her aide, a young man from Kenya, was so sweet with her that day. He would come to change her position, would smooth her gown, arrange her hands, and comb her hair. She must have weighed only 70 pounds.

We were all together when our deacon gave her last rites. It was wonderful how she talked to Veta, told her what we were doing and that she could let go. I felt so much more peaceful then.

Mom and I were alone with Veta after that, and my mom said that she had a story to tell me. While I was away on my trip, she'd received a call. The person identified himself as a used car salesman who sold the car my mother had traded in three-and-a-half years ago to a couple who gave it to their 16-year-old son. He is now 19 and in college in Michigan. He was cleaning the inside of the car when a ring fell to the ground. He saved it, brought it home to his parents, who called the car dealership. The salesman just happened to remember my mother, found her records and called her. Mom drove out to their house that weekend, and it was Veta's wedding ring. She gave it to me in Veta's presence the night she died.

Veta had a generous soul. There was never a time when she raised her voice to me. Never a time I felt rushed or unlistened to. And there was never a time that I left her home that she didn't say, "Now before you leave, look around, do you see anything you want?" I used to tease her that I couldn't compliment her on anything or she would give it to me. How fitting that this ring, the only item I'd ever wished to have to remember her by was returned that very night. I cannot help but think there was some divine intervention involved, that Veta made sure I got that ring back.

Veta died at 10:05 that night. Regretfully, I was at home, as was my mom. But I know Veta wasn't alone. And I know she was ready to go. Veta was always a private person, a dignified person. It is fitting that she would die in private. Now, I look forward to remembering her as she was, before she was sick. I have all of the letters she wrote me, and years of daily journals. I can read them now, in the quiet of my days, and think of her, and be grateful she was an influential part of my life.

Jo Ann Stanley

I'm looking at a photo of my mother and my daughter from my daughter's baby album. It's close to Christmas—baby's first Christmas. There's a tree with white bows and red balls, a gift underneath. Baby is wearing a red dress with lacy frills, white tights and red booties. She's looking up into her grandmother's face and my mother, wearing a Christmas corsage of carnations, smiles down at her granddaughter with all her characteristic warmth and kindness.

But wait—there's something wrong with this picture. My mother is sitting in a wheelchair. She's wearing a blue robe over her hospital gown. And her hair is gone.

My mother is not a cancer survivor. She died of the disease a short four months after this picture was taken, a year after she first found the lump in her breast that prompted a mastectomy. But today—I ask myself how she managed to survive that year. And how she managed to do so with such dignity and beauty.

Here's another photo of my mom from that terrible year, wearing that wig I hate. Her face looks worn and her smile is tired, a bit turned down at the corners. Her eyes appear small, her cheeks hollowed. She's sitting with her elder sister Helen, who was my mother's primary caregiver during the illness. I had a little baby then, and lived three hours away; when my aunt volunteered to stay with Mom, my siblings and I accepted with relief. Helen's sisterly love and devotion sustained my mother during the course of the disease. When my mother couldn't eat, my aunt learned how to give an IV of nutrients. When my mother couldn't read, her big sister read to her, just as she must have done when they both were children. When my mother couldn't walk, my aunt, though older, fetched and carried whatever she might need.

Here is another picture of the sisters from younger, happier days. They are both dressed in white for a formal portrait. Aunt Helen is a serious sixteen with a practiced smile and a short dark coif. My mom, nicknamed "Dolly," looks completely the part with light curls that have been trained into ringlets. She's only four years old, the baby of the family, with a sunny smile and shiny black shoes. Although there were two other siblings in between, my mother and her eldest sister shared a special bond since childhood that helped them to face the cancer together.

Here is one more photo of my mom, the one that inspires me every day. It's a black and white portrait in a silver frame. In this photograph my mother is a beautiful woman in her prime. Her hair rolls back from her high forehead and is tucked behind ears adorned with classic earrings. She looks like a movie star or maybe an airline stewardess with her tailored white collar and dark jacket. Her perfect skin, plucked eyebrows, and full lips suggest some artifice, but her eyes look into your heart and are serene. Her expression is a bit mysterious. No wonder my dad fell in love with her. I love the grace and style they both exhibit in their wedding portraits, and I treasure their obvious happiness. My dad died of a sudden heart attack about five years before my mother became ill. Like many loving spouses, my parents died within a few years of each other.

During her cancer, my mother suffered. She must have been afraid when she found that lump. She underwent the mutilation of mastectomy, but instead of recovering, she felt a new pain in her stomach. She had developed metastasized liver and pancreatic cancer. She was sick during chemotherapy, and lost all her hair. She was rewarded with a remission of three months' duration. From then on she was in and out of the hospital. My mother wanted to be at home, in her own bed, so Helen came and lived with her for two months, attending to her every need. My mother became weak, and even more ill. She needed medication for pain.

One night when the baby and I were staying with her she had a frightening psychological reaction to the medicine and woke in the middle of the night believing she was being attacked by robbers. I rushed downstairs where she was trying to unlock the door and escape into the night. It was very difficult to calm her down and get her back to bed. Another time when my brother and I took her to the doctor, he had to load the wheelchair in the trunk and carry her to the car. Her involuntary cries were from pain. After that, the doctors and nurses had to come to our home. One day I had to help my poor withered naked mother get out of the tub and back into her bed. After that we gave her sponge baths.

When I could be at home with Mom, I found we were reversing our old roles. I made her soup and grilled cheese sandwiches on days when she stayed in bed. When she couldn't eat, I fed her broth and gave her sips of water to keep her hydrated. I helped her swallow her medicine. Hospice came and made her more comfortable. Those last two weeks all the family gathered to be with her, never leaving her alone.

On the night she died, her sister was sleeping next to her. My aunt regrets that she did not wake up to witness the death. She feels guilty about it. She wanted to hold my mother's hand and tell her how much she loved her. But I believe my mother slipped from sleep to death so peacefully that no one could have heard her go.

In the last year of her life, my mother's chance of survival was as thin as a thread in a gossamer web. But her spirit was strong. She spoke optimistically with all the family. She looked ahead, organizing all of her papers while she was able, and carefully explaining all her affairs and desires. She took the time to label gifts with a friend or relative's name. She spoke about her ideas for a memorial service. She told us stories of her past that we had never heard before. She attended church services while she was still able and later, rested in her personal relationship with God. She spoke of her faith, how for many years she had thought of the afterlife as a "fairy tale," but how she now saw heaven on the horizon. She did not complain even when we knew she was in pain. She always thanked those who assisted her, never taking her due for granted. She faced her treatments, her pain, her losses and finally her death, with courage and dignity. When it came, my mother's death was a necessary release from the only, now horrible, alternative: survival.

Six Months to Live

IF

I think, said Christopher Robin, that we ought to eat all our provisions now,
so we won't have much to carry.

A. A. Milne

Patricia Antonopoulos

This fantasy flight will take off, but the landing might not be that expected disclaimer, the one that validates life as is, proclaiming the final six months a continuation of the status quo.

Maybe not.

First order of business is moving in a giant dumpster, a time to finally give up that insecurity that saves pieces of just-in-case life string. Time to give myself six months of a futureless sense of organized space.

Bob gets six months of weather, sports, and food talk, insuring easy avoidance of real conversations. Without future, what would be the point of sharing who we are?

My family would come every Sunday without exception, eating, laughing, enjoying together. This bit of magic we are weaving would require forgiveness, universal and complete. As long as enchantment has six-month magic, I would wear something beautiful on these Sundays, replacing the denim of everyday.

Coffee would be constant, strong, fresh and very hot. Not because I needed the boost, but simply because. Desserts become appetizers, rich and delicious, often cheesecake, sometimes chocolate.

An ounce of bourbon poured over a tall glass of ice would end each day as I read *To Kill a Mockingbird* over and over and over. I need to believe in the heroism of an Atticus Finch.

Television would totally disappear from my final six months. Evening hours would be filled with chosen things—walks, friends, conversations, books, family games, porch time watching the world go by.

Now to that disclaimer.

IF the six months were mine to orchestrate, no matter where they came in my life span, I would cherish such days. And in the interest of a thorough disclaimer, I just might...

act as silly as my grandchildren could tolerate,

learn to dance,

wear wild socks every day,

and always honor each need to laugh or to cry.

Patti Dickinson

I would snuggle with Wood every morning
I would throw the alarm clock away
I would swing on the swings
I would go off the high dive
I would stop buying floss
I would nap on rainy afternoons
I would walk on the beach, looking for shells and driftwood
I would do karaoke
I would be brave enough to say my goodbyes
I would throw away the bathroom scale
I would drink chocolate milk
I would take back the job of mowing the lawn from my teenagers
I would get a sheepdog
I would make my kids promise to keep the photo album caught up
I would have fresh flowers in every room of the house
I would ice skate
I would plant a cutting garden
I would sleep in the tree house with the kids

Shawna Samuel

There is a country song called "Live Like You're Dying." You know, "I'd go sky diving, Rocky Mountain climbing." Sounds simple. Then life gives you a real-life example or two of up-close and personal living while you're dying. Could be a child who loses her battle with cancer. Could be a friend, a neighbor who, despite grim odds, continues to look for any avenue that could lead to healing, no matter what the cost. Isn't it easy to say "Live Like You're Dying."? But what does it mean?

I have simplistic moments when I think that I'd just pitch all responsibilities, all material items and head to a beach. Sit in a chair by the ocean and enjoy the rest of the time I had left. What a shame to spend the last of your life in doctors' offices. Waiting in line for the MRI machine. Waiting for the doctor to spend his five minutes with you so he could quickly dispense the latest news, which will so sharply alter the course of your future, if you even have a future. But many of us do that.

And wouldn't I?

Wouldn't I stay and fight? Wouldn't I continue to do the laundry, shop for food, organize my house and change the sheets if I could? Wouldn't I choose to hold onto the life I actually have? And wouldn't the small things, the satisfaction of being in and enjoying the home I've made be the most valuable of all?

It seems like so much of life is ordinary: fulfilling obligations, duties, responsibilities like raising the kids, earning the grocery money. But what is the lesson here? Could it be that performing your ordinary tasks, your work, is and should be where the true source of joy comes from? Do we work hard all year just to escape for a few weeks on vacation, or do we enjoy that vacation because on it we can celebrate the life we get to go home to?

So many of us work harder and faster, thinking that just around this next bend, over this next hurdle, we'll be able to slow down and enjoy life. After this project is complete, after I get the next promotion, when this volunteer job is over. Thinking about what I would do if I only had six months to live has made me realize that that is all wrong. This is the day, with all the duties and responsibilities in it, where the true joy comes from. We're all missing the boat if we think the best part is just around the next corner. Live in the moment, celebrate all of its ordinariness, all of its joy. Because if it was taken away, you would fight like hell to get it all back.

Jo Ann Stanley

I I had six months to live, I would want to spend it in John's garden, the way John did.

John's death sentence was actually a year. One day he had some pain he couldn't explain, and pretty soon after that, maybe a week, the doctors told him he had incurable liver cancer. For quite some time, for months in fact, he was able to continue his daily activities. Only the last few months were those confined to the garden.

John's garden is in southern California, where all is lush and tropical. He has a lemon tree, birds of paradise, overgrown geraniums and a small lawn of bright green grass where his dog likes to play. Bougainvillea of the intense magenta variety snakes up the adobe walls of the garage. A square table with chairs seeks the sun and a round set lounges in the shade. Together they provided John with comfortable places for eating, drinking, or reading. Eventually, however, John spent more time on the edge of his garden than in it. His family moved his bed out to the veranda so that he could see the garden by day and the sky by night. But even in the starlight I think John could see the lemons on the tree.

"The lemon tree's essences loose in the moonlight. . . the lemons like stars in the tree's planetarium . . ." What are those lines from Neruda's *Elemental Odes*? Those poems could have been written in John's garden.

I don't mean to romanticize John's pain. His pain was real, his suffering acute. The cancer gnawed at his liver and aggressively attacked other organs in his diminishing frame. It became difficult to move, eat, think, or breathe. His beautiful wife, her wonderful parents, his lifelong friends—none had the ability to overcome or transcend that pain with anecdotes of happier days. In the end, only morphine could provide any respite. People could keep John company, feed, bathe, and love him, but they couldn't stop lucidity from slipping away. Near the end, he did say he was ready to die. That message was quite clear. We had to let him go.

John's garden was no Eden. But as in Eden, there was good and evil there. John himself was a good man. Sure, he was wild and crazy in his younger days. He actually earned his living as a private eye! He loved racing motorcycles and wouldn't quit for his wife's sake. He lived life with grand gestures. He had some pretty incredible encounters with lowlifes. Who could predict that something as boring as cancer would come to claim John? He had courted a quick if violent death, not a drawn-out illness that ate at him from the inside out. (In case you haven't guessed, the illness was the evil thing in the garden.)

It sounds terrible, doesn't it? So why would I want to spend my last six months in John's garden? I think I say that because the whole time he languished there, John was loved. For every difficult moment there was another of beauty, of spirituality, or dignity.

After John died, his friends and family gathered in the garden to remember him and to celebrate his life. We played the music he loved, ate and drank, and laughed about "the time that. . ." and "the time when. . ." His spirit there was strong.

If ever I face such an implacable foe, will I rise to the occasion as John did in John's garden? I doubt it, but I want to.

WHAT I KNOW FOR SURE

The Road is Forked

Life is so hard because it gives us the test first, then the lesson.

—Unknown

Patricia Antonopoulos

Cannot find it. Cannot find that place where I should be sheltering what I truly know. Know that it isn't where it was five years ago and certainly not where it was 25 years ago. Fifty-five years ago? Not even close.

The Bible has The Eight Beatitudes and I work to believe in them, but struggle because there is no evidence that they are true more often than not. St. Francis has that beautiful prayer but I must be resisting the channel.

There are times when I believe in "Act AS IF. . ." but that is eating snow. Looks beautiful, fluffs out nicely, seems refreshing and is always empty.

I know that churches have no need to build universities promulgating doctrine based on "My God's Better Than Your God". Fighting over married clergy, the role of women, gay marriage should be flyspecks. Church, as a place of refuge, a place where human needs are met is enough.

One of my strongest beliefs is the concept of family, people joined in a loving relationship of nurture and protection. That family is the best place for children to be raised, day by day by day in their own loving home.

Wonder how we got to the place that it takes two incomes to fulfill the American dream? Wonder how the dream became more stuff than substance?

I know that saying "I love you" has absolutely zero chance of universal meaning. I believe that many marriages die for lack of definition.

Could be that I am writing in dinosaur-speak, the almost universal condition of aging where we confuse wrinkles with wisdom. However, I do know it is time to take back our children, our young people. . . time to rescue them from the society we allowed to happen. I absolutely know that children have been grossly devalued as we have traded down, exchanging them for entertainment.

Beaver Cleaver and The Brady Bunch did not happen exactly as written, but better those models than the ones we allow in our homes today. I am certain that I do not know how to walk in a way that will influence any change. And, to make it sadder, I mistrust those who say they do know.

The one thing I know, not lost or hiding, is as close as I come to an absolute. People matter more. Family matters most.

Patti Dickinson

*T*here is NOTHING worse than a male recovering from anything medical.

It is ALWAYS chilly and raining on Halloween

The minute I do the change-of-season clothing switch, or wash all the winter coats, there is a 100 percent guarantee of a blizzard.

Laughing, until your sides hurt, is essential.

Human beings are not likely to be rehabilitated in our prisons.

I am very afraid for this generation of children, many of whom have been warehoused in day care.

Road rage is uncivilized and we'd better figure out what it's about.

You can't fight genetics.

Everyone should have a front porch.

Men and women are wired differently.

Neil Diamond touches my soul.

When I look back on my life, I really wouldn't change one single thing.

You can't have it all at the same time.

Moms and Dads shouldn't try to be friends with their kid(s).

Hollywood just doesn't get it.

I do my best sleeping when it rains or thunders.

When I dump dry spaghetti noodles in boiling water it NEVER looks like enough, and so I add more.

We are not very good in this culture at preparing people for death.

Shawna Samuel

I know for sure:

That I'm an eternal optimist, which has more good points than bad, but still has its drawbacks.

That life has its ups and downs.

That everyone has a cross to bear, challenges to overcome.

That marriage has its ups and downs, close times and distant ones, love and contempt, and that sometimes it's a fine line between the two.

That when the phone rings, I more often than not think that it's something fun to do, not something bad that's happened. And that when the phone rings, sometimes non-stop, it makes me realize that I'm fully engaged in life, and that that's a good thing.

An occasional rainy day does the soul good, but too many in a row can wreck havoc with one's mood.

Shutting my eyes in the sun is one of life's greatest pleasures.... Wrinkle worries be damned.

That cats are one of God's very best inventions.

That wearing nail polish and using really great soap are two of life's most affordable and most enjoyable luxuries.

That I'm capable of achieving a great deal in my life. That I have leadership abilities and talent that has gone untapped. That I'm on the brink of big changes and perhaps the very best part of my life. And that it thrills me and scares me equally. That it's scary to have something to prove.

That I've never earned a salary equal to the blood, sweat and tears I've given. That I want to earn that salary, finally.

That it scares me that earning a salary is a goal.

That change is hard.

That change is good.

That friends, family and love are the most important aspect to a happy life.

That balance of work and fun, giving to the outside world, and reflecting on your inside world is the secret to life. And that it's hard to do, but worth the effort.

That looking outside yourself, giving to something other than yourself is also key to happiness.

That people who love their work have it made.

That the most important blessing you can be given is health.

That I eat for comfort and reward, not always for hunger.

That exercise is one of the best things you can do for your mind, mood and body, yet it's the first thing to go in a busy schedule.

That women are many times selfless, to their detriment.

That wrinkles and wider bottoms are never a detriment to a friend's beauty, but can be all you see of yourself.

That the theory of forbidden fruit is one of the truest theories, and most difficult to overcome.

That stretching oneself with new challenges is one of the most important things to keep you vital, exciting and always learning. Yet it is one of the hardest things to continue to do in life.

That becoming a mother changes you forever. That it is the most wonderful thing that hurts the most in life.

There is hardly anything better than having your kids play creatively and actively together while visiting with a friend.

That women who stay home to raise their children are lucky…and have the toughest jobs of anybody.

Some things are worth doing halfway.

Some rules are meant to be broken.

That I know almost three pages worth of stuff.

Jo Ann Stanley

*W*hat I know for sure is less and less. For example, I'm taking a shower, and I'm ready to get out, and then I can't remember if I've soaped up or not. Or, I'm in the ATM line for ten minutes. It's my turn finally, and as I pull up I realize I've forgotten my PIN number. I feel like a safecracker trying different combinations, hoping for a lucky strike. Some days I've driven away penniless. Eventually, it comes back to me, and I get my cash reward.

Recently I read a terrifying article in the newspaper about the incidence of Alzheimer's as the Baby Boomer generation ages. Something like a third of us will develop the disease. I have to admit I worry sometimes about already being in the developmental stages. Factoids? Slipping. Celebrities? Dated. Crossword puzzle? Taking too long. Retrieving a name from my memory bank used to be so simple and automatic that I didn't even realize there was a process involved. Now my mind acts like an antiquated jukebox. The arm travels back and forth, searching, searching for the record and finally makes a selection. Then the music plays.

What's the name of that movie with that movie star? Julie. Not Julie Andrews. Andrews was in "Climb Every Mountain". This Julie was in the Russian movie. Not Anna Karenina. Was it Dr. No? I remember her muff. This is a new movie. Anyway, everyone says it's beautifully done, but I'm afraid to see it, because it's about Alzheimer's.

See how long it took me to retrieve the (faulty) data? And how imperfect the result? My stream of consciousness keeps bumping into rocks on its way down the mountain. But this memory loss issue isn't anything I've discussed with my doctor. Mentioning the topic might make it more real. Within the family, it's kind of a joke—we call my blips "senior moments." But is it only that?

I'm not a hypochondriac. But as I age it's not only the little aches and pains that bother me more. It's the fear of dementia battling with the potential lump in my breast.

LIFE STORIES

Rivers of Remembrance

When we write from experience, we harvest our lives.

——**Bonnie Goldberg**

Patricia Antonopoulos

Nature gave the chameleon the ability to blend, to disappear into the background. Without conscious decision, the creature becomes whatever is needed to physically survive.

My life displays chameleon behavior in blending, in moving quietly away, in guarding against emotional loss.

A kindergarten memory is clear. I became a marshmallow, soft and white, so noise could not come from me. Mrs. Unger could not single out my footfalls.

Elementary school was a conscious decision to excel. My parents expected a report card filled with 95 or above in every subject, especially the dreaded DEPORTMENT. That score had to be 100 percent or there were questions about what behavior was causing the downgrade. The nuns and priests valued excellence in academic work, modesty in behavior, and straight-line religion. Behold the over-achiever, bleached to blend!

Our clothing, uniforms often included, came hand-me-down from a neighbor. An ugly air-deprived-blue coat kept me warm through several winters, unless the coat spent the school day hidden under a bush, my new camo-color.

During those winters I saved money earned helping neighbors do chores. Finally, I had enough saved for beautiful off-white wool and black buttons. Mom made the long coat with a hood and put what she called "graduated buttons" down the front. The first time I wore the new coat was to Thursday night church service. Someone asked if we couldn't afford buttons of all the same size. . . fade to background.

Slumber parties or spending the night with a friend were agony. The giggling, the girl rituals just did not fit and I often found myself walking home before 10:00 p.m., red-faced and confused.

My mother had a full time job. It was the 1950s and none of our friends or neighbors had moms who worked outside the home. Mom's working was considered a sign that my Dad could not provide with his income.

My older brother had a job at a grocery store so he could pay for needed orthodontic work. The care of the house came to me and to my sisters. We all had our jobs. If anything were left undone, Mom's anger was so difficult that I made a decision to do as many jobs as I could so that the anger did not happen.

The girls' bedroom had a very large closet that followed the slant of the roof and narrowed to a hiding cave at the back. When my mother was angry—kitchen work that didn't measure up, a uniform tie with a spot of lunch soiling it, a carpet not vacuumed—I would wait for the anger to vent. Then I would go to the cave. It was the gray place, the place to cry.

When I was 14, I knew that I was in love with Bob. He had been my brother's friend for over a year and spent many hours in the basement workshop. The amount of gingerbread with lemon sauce that I baked and carried to that workshop was unbelievable. Finally, we went for a walk and were happily taking walks for the next two years. My parents acquiesced, but never really accepted. We were too young.

During my senior year, Bob was in the Army and I stayed focused on school. He came home on leave and we seemed to quarrel more than we went for walks. He saw no need for college. I could not imagine giving up the joy of learning in a school setting. I enrolled in college. My relationship with Bob ended.

During the first year of college, a priest had asked the three females enrolled in his logic class to withdraw from the class. His experience told him that we were unsuited to excel in logic. That is the first time I remember making a decision based on iron-willed determination to prove someone wrong. This time, I would be golden.

When Father Fiola handed me my final paper and my final grade, both A+, he smiled and said, "God has given you a gift and HE has great things planned for you." This is my first awareness that to some people, my successes were due to God's grace and my failures were due to my lack of cooperation with that grace. An apology from him would have been nicer.

My dad had always wanted me to be a Catholic Sister of Charity, a nun. He pushed hard. He had always maintained that we could go to college if we paid for it and we would live at home until we married. It never occurred to me that I would counter those decisions.

Now I was 18, dreaming of completing college and listening to Dad tell me of his dream for me that began at my birth. My job in the office of a hospital and the babysitting money were not going to be enough to supplement the scholarship to St. Mary College.

A Navy veteran returning to college enrolled at the same college. He asked me out. We dated for over a year and he talked about a plan. We would marry, I would work to put him through college and then I would finish college. During a lunch break at school, he gave me an engagement ring. That evening, I showed the ring to my dad and his disappointment was overwhelming. "It is not too late." he said. "You can give it back and wear the habit."

This life-changing decision was based on my need to go to college, to leave my parent's home, and to NOT be an old maid. I was still 18. At 19, we were married. At 20, I was pregnant and my son was born ten-and-a-half months after the wedding date. The moment of his birth was monumental. That joy is fresh today. This beautiful moment blessed my life four more times as my other children were born during the next seven years. Rainbows were real.

Thirteen months after my son's birth, my daughter was born after an extremely difficult pregnancy complicated by measles. I had been told that she would be blind, deaf and possibly mentally retarded. She stayed in the hospital for about three weeks. During that time, her dad fell and injured his ankle. A nightmare began. Without anyone's knowledge he was seeing several doctors and getting various pain pills. His behavior reflected the awful power of drugs on the brain.

Within seven-and-a-half years, I had five children and was immersed in being Mom. He taught high school and worked part time in a grocery store. I was unbearably lonely, but knew that loneliness was not acceptable in my circumstances. So I worked at being the perfect Mom and the perfect housekeeper, taking whatever part-time work would bring in money and allow me to be at home with my children. Finishing college would wait.

During those years, I loved the time with my kids, yet I ached for companionship, for adult friendship. We had no mutual friends. His discipline of the children was harsh.

After my third child was born, the marriage had become unbearably damaged. One evening I took the kids out to the car for a visit with Papa and Nana, my parents. Before he went to bed, their dad had taken the distributor cap off the car so I could not go anywhere. I counted the money in my purse and walked with the kids to the bus stop. The bus got to 12th and Main, a downtown area. The driver said he was heading for the car-barn. We had to get off and take another bus. A transfer was not good for the next part of the ride and I did not have enough money for a second fare. I called my dad to come pick us up.

While the kids played in my parent's family room, I asked my dad if I could live at home for a short time until I found a job and an apartment. Mom sat mute through this conversation. Finally, my dad said no—I should go home and stay with my marriage vows. Pages could be written here, but that was then, not now. Dad drove us back to our house.

When my youngest child was in kindergarten, I enrolled at UMKC and began working towards finishing my education degree. Those years are encased in a haze, but I know they were most difficult for Chris. His young life had too much structure when playing was his right. The perfectly clean house, the less than perfect Mom (but trying), and the college student melded into a time of stress and fatigue. If I wanted to do this, it was my challenge and my responsibility.

Shawnee Mission School District hired me in 1974 and I began teaching kindergarten and working on a master's degree. My much-loved grandfather, Pop, died and I missed him terribly.

This time period was intense. I loved being Mom and I loved teaching. The other side of my life was filled with a rebelling teen-age son, and intense anger at my husband. Our family was cracking. We tried family counseling but after a few sessions my husband refused to go. Finally, the therapist told us that because the problem stayed home, we needed to discontinue the therapy.

My dad died a slow and painful death, losing the fight with cancer. My sisters and I took on the new role of caretaker for our mom. One son, angry, moved away.

After 23 years, I made a decision to leave the marriage. This is a decision I revisit constantly because of the effect on my children. I rationalized that they were old enough to understand. They were not. They felt abandoned. They were harmed. There is no undoing a divorce. For whatever good comes from ending a marriage, children suffer. My regret is very real.

During the time after the divorce, I was on a high school class reunion planning team and we were planning a multiple class reunion, inviting those from three consecutive years. Bob's name was on my calling list. When we met again, we started going for walks. We were married in a simple ceremony on a Wednesday in a small church in Platte City, Missouri. My youngest son, Chris, was our best man.

These were difficult years for all of us. My children's father died in his high school classroom shortly before the students arrived. A colleague came into the room while the stroke was happening, but it was too late. My oldest son, Mark, called to tell me of the death and some of the stored pain let go. Sadly, their father died before the first grandchild was born.

My youngest son had open-heart surgery. These were unbearable days and weeks, the worst time of my life.

My mother's stroke and her need for care was the final addition to a growing list of reasons for an early retirement from my "home" for 22 years. The people of my elementary school, the staff and parents, had been a life anchor through so many storms. The care and concern given to me through those years saved much of what is now me. But I had to release that haven and move into a new phase. Mom lived for about two-and-a-half years and we were at her side when she died, November 28, 2000.

The writing of my life story was completed some time ago. I need to end with my JOY.

My children, Mark, Elizabeth, Paul, Dan, and Chris, my grandchildren, Cain, Molly, Frank, and Sam, daughters-in-law Kaiya, Ida and Kristi, and my life with Bob have revitalized my connection to joy and given me renewed purpose. Time with them is precious beyond words.

Restoring and refreshing my relationship with my siblings has been affirming. New and sustaining friends have added a fresh dimension of joy. All of these people created a gift for me, the gift of my life.

Patti Dickinson

*A*life story—a daunting task. Condensing the years. Sifting memories. What's relevant? What brought me to the place I am now? So many foggy memories. So many memories like just yesterday.

My mother, the youngest of five children. My dad the youngest of two. A storybook couple. They looked like they should go together. My mother was on the cover of *Life* magazine, dancing with a cadet from Annapolis. I was born in June of 1953, the first child of Jeanne and Don Shea. Three years later my brother, Don, was born. I still remember his homecoming. He lay on the couch, and as I approached, adults screamed, "Be careful of him." At five, I went to kindergarten. Mrs. Diederich was my teacher. Had the measles. Still can remember sleeping in a dark room, with pigtails matted to my head, through days of foggy slumber.

Third grade. Took pencils to school to donate to the missions for pagan babies. Decided to keep them. Sharpened every one of them, and proudly used them to do perfect, Catholic school Palmer-method handwriting. Never got caught. Still appalled that I did that.

Fifth grade. Kennedy was shot. Had a nun that year that I wished every single night was my mother. She was plump, like pillows. Could just imagine what it would be like to cuddle with her, reading stories, or just talking. Handwriting was still a big deal. I sat next to a girl named Laura who had a maroon fountain pen, not a standard-issue Shaffer, but one that was solid maroon, no tacky clear barrel. She had the most beautiful handwriting. She was left-handed, so that's what I became. (Although my handedness had been established years earlier, as a "definite right.") Seventh grade. My younger brother was a mess. Too many moves. Too many schools. Too many failed attempts to make friends. Vivid image of my mother smirking at the dinner table one evening. She looked over at my plate and told me that I needed to eat the butter that I took that didn't melt on the vegetables I'd already eaten. I couldn't even eat unmelted butter on toast. She knew that. So I compliantly put the butter in my mouth and willed it to slither down my throat uneventfully. Nope. Wasn't working. I reached for my milk, thinking I could wash it down. I was terrified. Gulping for air, heart banging in my chest. Why did she treat me this way? I took a swig of milk, and knew that it wouldn't go down. I ran for the bathroom and vomited. I returned to the table, humiliated. No one spoke.

Eighth grade in Riverdale, New York. Chased across a footbridge spanning Henry Hudson Parkway by John Ryan, asking me to go steady. Heart pounding (out of fear, not love); he never caught me. He didn't think that half the fun was the pursuit, because he decided to pursue Diane Robinson, a very curvaceous peer, with Farrah Fawcett blonde hair and a restrained, but implied sensuality to her—she oozed hormones even in a plaid, Catholic school jumper.

I went to three high schools. Began at Our Lady of Victory in Dobbs Ferry, New York. Moved to Kansas City in the middle of my freshman year. Finished my freshman year at Sion, and spent sophomore year there. Lots of girl friends. I was on the Student Council and was considered a lot of fun at slumber parties. April 25, 1969, Mary McGee fixed my best friend Susan and me up with blind dates for a school mixer. Wood went with Susan, I was with Brian Boeding. We spent about five hours together, during which time we exchanged about twenty words. And I said nineteen of them. The next day Wood called me and asked me out. Dated through the summer of 1969. My dad announced at the end of the summer that we were moving to Houston. I was one angry teenager, but internalized every shred of the rage. I did not act out, other than experimentation with Tareyton cigarettes and a very bad experience with Schlitz Malt Liquor. Once. You don't want the details. No drugs, no promiscuity. Just an internally coming-apart-at-the-seams teen. Three high schools in as many years. Parents' marriage on the rocks. Talk of divorce. Scared. Mad. Trying to help my parents patch it together. But not too sure that I wanted them to if it meant we didn't all have to move.

We moved. Wrong choice. My parents still arguing. Felt wrenched out of a school I was happy in, to listen to my mother's well-timed jabs at my dad and play voyeur to such intentional disrespect. But even worse was the cold silence that screamed of the lack of love. Had my fill. Hindsight tells me that I played the role laid out for me—I met all expectations. I was the quintessential good kid. Too compliant, too easy going, I was the adult holding it all together at fifteen. Fortunately I'd met the right boy, who didn't cash in on my vulnerabilities. He was my friend first, in every sense of the word. He listened so openly. He didn't judge. He didn't "fix" it. No one could have fixed this mess, but he didn't try. I didn't need a boyfriend at this point. My life was too complicated for a boyfriend. I was hanging on by a thread. I was living with two adults, one who was emotionally abusive to my dad and emotionally unavailable to her children. Memories of this period feel sterile. I remember little family conversation. Little warmth. No one telling me to study. No one cared if I did or didn't.

Had a wonderful late twenty-something high school English teacher, Miss Cramaris, who took me under her wing. I was writing some very bad poetry at this time--she'd have me over to her apartment on Saturday mornings so I could share it with her. She probably saved me from coming totally undone. She made me feel smart, valued. My parents never questioned my coming and going with this woman.

I was college-bound, not because I had any burning interest in doing much of anything specific, but because that was what the other sixteen of my classmates were busy doing. My mother thought St. Edward's University in Austin was a great choice—small, Catholic, sheltered. I had my sights set on the University of Texas at Austin. I won only because the tuition was so much cheaper. Forty thousand plus students. A "real" college campus. I decided to major in English. Wood was headed for T.C.U. in Fort Worth. We would soon be three hours apart, door to door.

I roomed with a high school friend in Littlefield, an all-freshman dorm on campus. Un-air-conditioned. Blistering heat. Spent my first semester playing spades in the hall of the dorm. I had a lot of friends. After the first semester it was time to get serious about academics. My parents weren't too concerned. Pretty indifferent. Did well the next semester. I liked Austin, had a nice circle of friends.

I had a friend named Annette. She lived right across the hall from me— grew up in Austin on a turkey farm, just outside the city limits. Since the dorm didn't serve dinner on Sunday nights, I often got invited to dinner. I went every single time I was asked. Huge spread. Cats, dogs, kittens everywhere. A barn full of turkeys, gobbling. Chickens, too. Huge farmhouse table, huge bowls of mashed potatoes, vegetables, homemade bread. THREE kinds of pie for dessert. This was living. Good conversation, lots of laughing, camaraderie. It was at this moment that I knew that I wanted to create this atmosphere with my not-yet-created family. I always was so sad when it was time to go back to the dorm. I hated leaving this nest. There was a comfort level here. A safety.

Was seeing Wood about every other weekend. He'd drive from Fort Worth on Friday afternoons, and he'd stay until dinnertime Sunday. Our relationship was exclusive. I've often thought that we were fortunate that we grew together in the same direction. I think that's probably pretty unusual. I wouldn't recommend that sort of dating relationship for any of my daughters. Wood was from a very dysfunctional home as well, the youngest of three boys. Two alcoholic parents. A brother who died at fifty-eight. He was one of the worst cases of Obsessive Compulsive Disorder that a psychiatrist friend of ours had ever seen. The depth of his "closet existence" was only discovered after his death.

My college days were probably benign by most standards. A few evenings out with friends where I drank too much beer, but no wild sexual exploits or drug experimentation. Not out of any sense of righteousness. I'm not a risk taker. But I was frightened of my mother and her conditional love. I knew, innately that I had no "wiggle room," that if I strayed, the consequences of my transgression would be dire. Years later, I was proven correct in my perception of her. I can remember The Who, one of Wood's and my favorite bands coming to Fort Worth and calling home for permission to go. "'No." No discussion. I was unhappy, but I was compliant.

Wood and I got engaged in May of my junior year in college. Wood was graduating in December, so we decided to marry in January of 1975. Then I'd only have one final semester to get through and we'd both be done, and move back to Kansas City where Wood was going to work for his dad.

Planning our wedding was pretty much a blur. I remember leaving Austin, driving the three hours to Houston to spend time picking out china, silver and crystal. I remember shopping for a rehearsal dinner dress. Standing in the dressing room as I tried on seemingly hundreds of dresses. At one point, totally frustrated, my mother literally threw her hands up, in the Sakowitz dressing room and said, big sigh first, "You're just not the dress type." Still today, twenty-seven years later, I wonder whether that is really so, or if it's now my perception that it's so because that's what I was told.

My relationship with Wood's parents was "pursed lips polite." Wood's dad was oftentimes seemingly befuddled in a Mr. Magoo sort of way. I can remember wondering how this man could be so successful. He certainly didn't seem like a crackerjack businessman, rubbing elbows with Hollywood types and bankers. Wood's mom was reserved—conversation with her was often stilted. She wanted a Junior League type for a daughter-in-law. I was sturdy. Smile. I remember being in their kitchen, visiting over Christmas break when we were still in high school and she'd just gotten a microwave oven. She cooked me a cinnamon roll. She proudly served it to me, and I took a bite and it tasted just like the ash, but in solid form, that would be left over in the bottom of the charcoal grill after cooking hot dogs. I had no prior experience with pending mothers-in-law, microwaves or eating microwaved-to-death food, so as she sat next to me, I ate every bite. It scored me no points.

Later in our marriage, after we had three or four kids, she really ramped up about me joining the Junior League and Fireside Committee, and many more such organizations that I've happily forgotten the names of. I politely declined. At one point, I remember being out to dinner with my in-laws at the Carriage Club and she started going over the same old stuff. I told her, pretty bluntly, that I was a busy mom, that I had many friends that I hadn't see in a while, and that I wasn't in the market for NEW friends. That seemed to get the message across. The rest of the meal was chilly. Perhaps it's a generational thing, but I am much more a "roll up my shirtsleeves" type. She was happy to write a check and do committee work. Both have their place, but philosophically, we were miles apart.

Wood and I spent two years in Kansas City before Wood decided to go back to Fort Worth and get his master's degree in Radio-TV-Film. He got a full-tuition scholarship with a stipend that allowed us to live in a dump and supplement with our savings. Wood's parents had no idea about our plans, so we went over there for dinner one night, with the idea that Wood would tell them that we were moving back to Texas. The last thing I said as we walked in the kitchen door was, "Honey, don't tell them over the salad, wait until dessert." Before I had the first lettuce leaf speared, Wood was telling his parents our plans. It was frigid around that table. I couldn't get out of there fast enough.

Off we went. Wood loved the program, the people, the opportunity. He won a few awards. Satisfying, gratifying. I was working on teacher certification. We loved the life we were living. Being students suited us. We had about four couples we ran around with on weekends, who were as broke as we were. None of us had kids. These friends were the crew/actors/actresses for Wood's thesis film. Many wonderful memories from this time.

Back to Kansas City. We were ready to start a family. We'd been married for three years. Eighteen months later, we'd gotten a lot of practice trying. Went to my ob, and we were now on the infertility track. Wood was told to bring in a sperm sample. On a bitter cold day in the middle of January, Wood took his sample in, after running several errands on the way over there, and leaving the sample in the car. Grim news. No motility, way too few million to ever conceive. He was ordered in to repeat the "procedure." This time they wanted him to give it in the office. He said there was a nice selection of magazines in the room. Hmmm. He passed. I was temperature queen, but I never plotted a dip before the rise, which to you rookies who have never been through this ridiculous maze, means you're ovulating. I have had just about every obstetric horror done to me, in the attempt to achieve pregnancy. The endometrial biopsy that the O.B. told me would be a "little pinch," for example. It ought to be illegal to do that procedure without a general anesthetic. The laparoscopy was next. Found out that I only had one ovary and one fallopian tube, so I was ovulating every other month. Swell. That just cut down the odds by 50 percent. Now what kind of a miracle did we need?

I got a job teaching at our Lady of the Americas on the West Side of Kansas City, Missouri. I taught kindergarten in the morning, sixth grade in the afternoon. Left there and went to teach at Brookridge Day School. I taught an all-day kindergarten. The Sunday paper came out with a big spread on adoption, complete with attorneys' names. We sent a letter to one of the attorneys. He called and wanted to interview Wood and I. At the end of the interview, in January, 1981, he told us to write a check for $50 to our favorite charity and leave it with him. No charge for the interview. Thought it would be years until we heard from him. We heard on May 1, 1981. Matt was born, a healthy baby. The mother wanted a Catholic family and we were the only Catholic family on his list.

My mother-in-law was very supportive of our fertility quest, my mother was not. "You don't know what you're getting." Or, "Is being a parent really THAT big a deal?" My insecurities were very high with my mom; I'd find myself second-guessing myself, wondering if maybe it WAS time to stop all this fertility stuff and move on.

We embraced being new parents. We knew pretty quickly that we'd like to do this again. We got that chance two and a half years later, on the evening of December 4, 1983. Matt bundled up in his snowsuit, Wood looking for the car keys so we could go and buy our Christmas tree. The phone rang, and I answered. An attorney neighbor of ours. She had a baby girl that they were trying to place with neighbors of ours who were also trying to adopt. They were in the midst of doing a foreign adoption through Gentle Shepherd and felt like they had thrown too much money in that direction to walk away. So they told the attorney to call us. Were we interested? Yes! The next day we had Elizabeth. She is the kid responsible for the family tradition of going for our Christmas tree every year on her birthday. Eighteen months later we did our third adoption, Claire. June of 1985. We knew we'd beat all the odds adopting three healthy newborns.

We weren't done beating the odds yet. Claire was about seven weeks old when I did an at-home pregnancy test and it came up positive. How could this be? We'd thrown away the thermometer, the sex on demand, on day 14-16-18. (Diane Robinson, eighth grade bombshell had nothing on me!) It was hard to get pregnant. I had three kids under the age of four and I was weary. My OB roared. The whole office celebrated. Kathleen was born May 9, 1985, during a thunderstorm. My parents came to watch the kids while I was in the hospital. Wood came home from the hospital to shower and change clothes and found his parents over there, drinking with my parents, and the kids running wild, unsupervised. Sigh.

This was perhaps one of the first times that Wood and I had a serious conversation about our collective parents' drinking. How it was affecting our trust in them, making us question their judgment in terms of our kids. How insidious alcoholism is. Three months later, at Kathleen's baptism, we had a major fallout with my mom. She was mildly annoyed that my college friend, Kathleen's godmother, had made her a christening dress. For the first three kids we'd used a family gown that was ripped, yellowed and being mailed back and forth amongst the cousins. I said to my mom, "Boy, what do you think I should do?" She told me, spitting the words, that she hadn't brought the family christening gown. So we used the new, handmade gown. Boy, I'd stepped in it now. She really had brought the gown. And I had not expressed any huge amount of regret that she hadn't. She didn't speak to me all weekend. Instead she drank. So on Sunday, I told her, in front of my brother, dad, and Wood that I thought that she was drinking too much and it was affecting her relationships. She never said a word, until I was done talking. Then she looked at my dad and said, "Get me a beer." That was the last time we saw my mother. Fifteen years ago. She has never met four of my children. We've probably seen my dad four times in these years. There aren't words to describe the feelings that I can't pull out into the light of day. Not now. Perhaps not ever. My mother terrifies me. I couldn't call her. I couldn't write. I have tried that in the past and I know how vindictive and mean she can be. She would belittle me. Tell me that this was my fault. And I just might, in a weak moment, wonder if it was.

Four more kids in the next ten years. We were done. I could now look at a baby in someone else's arms and not get that longing. Then boom. In 1999 Wood got a letter from a missionary in Chicago that sends crates of food and medical supplies to Romania. Wood said he would get the vendors that he knew to send candy and popcorn over. They sent group pictures of the children in return. Wood and I had been on a waiting list early on to adopt from Korea. Now we were considering adopting from Romania. Wood went to Romania in December of 1999 to pick up Dan and Tim, a five-year-old and nearly four-year-old.

Big mistake. It took us four months to realize just how big. These boys were, as a social worker friend of ours explained, like animals. Attachment disorders that they wouldn't grow out of. Tim had muscular dystrophy and no speech. Not in Romanian or English. Our pediatrician took one look at them and shook his head. Dan had many signs of sexual and physical abuse. Angry. Acting out. His preschool teacher said he was making Meghan miserable. This wasn't working. Wood wasn't talking, I was angry with his silence. I woke up one morning five months into this ordeal, getting no help from the agency, a pediatrician recommending that we return these boys to the agency and stood across the bed from Wood and said, "I can't do this anymore." Huge feelings of failure. What kind of mother gives them back?? What was wrong with me? Us? Our other kids? There was no connection. I looked at my two youngest and could see how badly this wasn't working. So we undid it. We found at attorney in town that specializes in disrupted adoptions. Within two weeks they were placed in two different homes. Such an incredible relief. Six months of such a disconnect from our family. We all reveled in it being just the original ten again.

In May,1999, our oldest son, Matt, graduated from Bishop Miege. A brilliant kid who never hit his stride. Underachiever. Sputtered to graduation. Headed off to be a sailor and seemingly never looked back. Got through basic training in Great Lakes, Illinois. We went for his graduation. All nine of us. He seemed so much older, taller, quieter. He was sent to Pensacola for Air Rescue Training. Jumping out of helicopters in the dark. A lot of physical endurance challenges. It seemed as though he was meeting the expectations. He got two weeks leave before he was to report to the John F. Kennedy Aircraft Carrier. Wood took him to the airport, and that's the last we heard.

Two months later, we did a health and wellness check through the Red Cross. An e-mail came back that he was on the ship, but unable to contact us. Three months later, still no word; we sent a package of letters in one manila envelope. It came back undeliverable five weeks later. Another health and wellness check and this time the news was grim, definitive. Matt had never reported. Ever. Thud. Disbelief, disappointment, anger, shame, intense feelings of failure, and overwhelming, crushing sadness.

I am much more adept at guilt than I am at sadness. And if I diminish who I am, which is what misplaced guilt is, then I don't have to diminish who HE is. I'm weary. But I'm sturdy. I mow. I sell carnival tickets. I help Margaret find "P" show and tells and make up three clues so the guessing game can happen in the classroom. I keep putting one foot in front of the other. I "do" so I don't have to unleash the emotions that scare me so. Right now the ugliness of rage is combining with defeat and despair and sadness. All of which I'm desperately trying to beat back with a stick. Unproductive, yes. But a lifelong pattern that needs lots of work. Lots of tears writing this story. Lots of walking away and coming back later. Matt has left Wood and me with a tall order—explaining to the family that he has abandoned his responsibility, and left us to muster the courage to tell our kids, our friends. I resent the wreckage he's left me to explain. I look at Andrew and wonder how I can tell him the sailor hat that he wore all the way home from Chicago after Matt's graduation from Boot Camp is now just a hat, no longer a symbol of his hero.

I know that God writes straight with crooked lines. Those are the words that I mutter when the despair seems to suffocate me.

I think, often, about the legacy that I'm leaving my kids. The troubles that I've had with Elizabeth and now Matt have made me much less judgmental. I now know that wayward teens—mine or someone else's—are spoken of in the same breath as, "There but for the grace of God go I."

Margaret, our youngest, went to kindergarten this year. I'm still trying to find my stride. Walking away from the kindergarten door isn't a whole lot easier now than it was three weeks ago. The sweater that I was going to finish knitting still isn't out of the closet. I am pursuing an interest in working with troubled kids. I went to the Topeka Juvenile Correctional Facility and the Topeka Women's Prison last summer as part of a class to renew teacher certification and discovered a passion that I didn't know I had. A life-altering experience. I am corresponding with Michael, an incarcerated nineteen-year-old young man whom I met while I was there. He is due to be released in late October.

The irony isn't lost on me. Michael is a tall, handsome, chisel-chinned kid that reminds me of Matt. This kid invades my sleep; maybe it's a second chance. I don't know. My words couldn't ever make an impact on Matt. Maybe they will affect Michael. I felt compelled to write a letter to the editor after visiting the juvenile facility. I will never be the same—lockdown, wire-inside-the-glass-windows, kids screaming, the sound reverberating off the institutional metal doors and dirty linoleum floors. Pain has a voice. These were someone's children. Crime has a face. And where, where was the village?

The segment of my story that is about Matt has been rewritten many times. Each time a little more honestly. Initially I told the heart of it, but the soul of it was not there. I think that emotionally, we pick what we are able to deal with, and beat back with a stick what we can't. And over time, that becomes a habit. And eventually, we never bring into the light of day the stuff that causes us too much pain, grief, shame, sadness. Those are the very things that brought me to tears as I wrote my life story. The emotional price of getting this story on paper was huge. I'm beginning to reevaluate some of those old tapes. The "get on with it" tape. It happened, it's over. Business as usual. But all those years I've left out the middle, so I'm trying to learn how to incorporate it into my life. I now know that the middle IS the soul of it.

We take the good and the not-so-good and make of it what we will. Because a very wise woman once said, "This story is all of our stories."

Shawna Samuel

*L*ove Child. My father was a freshman in college, my mother a sophomore, when they learned about me. I was the surprise that kept my dad out of Vietnam, and that allowed my parents, who had been sweethearts since eighth grade, to joyfully transfer to the same college, Wichita State, and marry. My father's mother, Veta, spent a great deal of time helping with me those first years as my parents finished school. By the time I was five years old, we moved to Kansas City, so my dad could work at Southwestern Bell in their marketing department. Apparently as we loaded ourselves in our small car for the trip to Kansas City, I scooted over, patted the seat next to me and told Veta that that spot was for her. I can only imagine how that smarted.

This was not the dream; this was what paid the bills. Before me, my father was majoring in forestry in Colorado, and had experience working in a vet's office. He loved the outdoors, animals, fishing, hunting and camping. My mom shared his love of animals, but was not a natural hunter and camper. So my dad continued to go with buddies, or alone. I had a normal, happy childhood, albeit without any brothers or sisters. I think my parents were always trying to get one leg up on their finances, and never felt the luxury to talk about extra children. Both of their parents had helped them financially, so they were paying debts from the beginning.

My childhood stopped seeming normal when my dad went fishing one weekend and never came back. His boat was hit by a drunk driver and he died. It took them three days to find his body. I was 11, and in between fifth and sixth grade. What was most devastating at the time, through the eyes of an 11-year-old, was watching the grief of my family. How could I possibly add to that? So I was strong. Our roles as mother and child were instantly and irrevocably reversed. My mother, after paralyzing grief, went back to school to get a degree in computer programming, something to pay the bills rather than the teaching degree she had earned in the '60s. I was alone a lot, and spent a great deal of time across the street at the neighbors' house. They were a retired couple, and were kind to me, until the man sexually molested me one day. End of extended family.

My mother discovered this by reading my diary that I had taped underneath a table in my room. She had known something was wrong. She was furious with me for not telling her. Her fury added to my guilt about the situation, which I felt was somehow my fault. I begged my mother not to pursue any recourse, and we swept it under the rug, pretending it didn't happen. The man was still invited to our house, and we to his. This, looking back, is one of my only serious regrets in my life. It was not the right choice. Not only did it leave me the victim, but his wife, who'd been so kind to me, never understood why I suddenly changed and turned cold.

To say that my mother handled being widowed poorly is unfair, for who could? But losing my dad devastated her, and she has never fully recovered. I felt the need, whether justified or not, to fill in some of the voids due to her loneliness. She felt crushing responsibility to raise me alone, so could be forcefully strict. In response, I was obstinate. But I was a good kid overall, made good grades, and was never in trouble. Nevertheless, it was a complicated and stormy adolescence, filled with fighting. I was, and still am, in many ways the parent. Difficult as those years were, I respect and admire my mother for not only making ends meet, but for giving me a fine education at a private university, an awesome accomplishment. Actually, I respect her for just putting one foot in front of the other. Who's to say I could have in her shoes.

Both of my parents were only children, so being the only child and grandchild was difficult. All of their eggs were in my basket. I heard more than once that if anything bad happened to me, they would die. Anxiety was our family's coat of armor. As the only child, I felt watched. Christmas morning, everyone would get all set up, including my grandpa's big reel-to-reel camera with a head of eight bright lights, I'd have my hair done perfectly, put on a new dress, and make an entrance into the living room, squinting like everyone else from the bright lights, to open my stocking with everyone watching. I felt the need to appreciate all they'd done, to pay everyone back for the kindness and generosity in the haul of presents I was about to dig into. Presents I would undoubtedly feel guilty for one way or another. There were some Christmas mornings I spent a while in the bathroom feeling like I was going to throw up. "Oh, she gets herself so excited." Yes, there was pressure being the only child for two generations. Duncan and I let our children open their Christmas stockings in their rooms, alone, when they first wake up. No watching. No expectations. Just giving, without any strings. It's my favorite part of Christmas day, hearing their uninhibited excitement from their rooms in the early dark of the morning.

For most of my childhood, I was an unpopular nerd, or teacher's pet. I always had a couple of really good friends, but never a crowd to run with, even though I dreamed of that. I was way too mature and goofy. But I finally hit my stride in high school when I found that I loved the theatre, got an office job, and met a nice boy. I loved working. Loved the independence. I had a steady boyfriend for the first few years of high school. Then, during senior year, I dated around and really had a blast. I wanted to go into television news, so I chose my college based on that, and the fact that I wanted it to be at least 500 miles away from home to help break the apron strings. I went to DePauw University in Indiana, a small, private, traditional liberal arts school.

Ironically, right before I left for college, I met Duncan, my husband. But even though I was leaving, he gave me all the room I needed in school; and I had a ball there, too. It was the first time in my life I decided to be totally myself—take it or leave it—no trying to fit in. My best friends, my friends for life, were made that first year of school. What do you know? Lesson learned. My relationship with Duncan developed slowly, at first through letters. We grew closer throughout the years, and he even escorted me to sorority dances as a 34-year-old. It was quite the talk of the sorority house.

Duncan and I married a year after I graduated from DePauw. My television news career started at KQTV-News in St. Joseph, Missouri, but quickly flowed into public relations at Twentieth Century Investments as the need for normal hours in the city where Duncan was settled pulled at my heart. I enjoyed my career very much until I had Caitlin, and retired.

The happiest time of my life has been while married. I love our children, our home, our pets, our community, our lives. We've had our ups and downs: challenges with infertility, a child with learning disabilities and parents and grandparents aging and dying. But after my childhood, what I love most of all about our lives is the normalcy. Our kids are having the fairy tale childhood I dreamed about and wished for. I was panicked to have a second child, as a guarantee that I wouldn't be a widow with a single daughter like my mom. How ironic that I would fall in love with an older man.

My father and I were much alike, in physical characteristics, mannerisms, and our sense of humor. He was so young and strong, in the prime of his life when he died. It doesn't seem possible that an accident could take him. I'm now ten years older than he ever got to be. And in some ways, I feel I'm cheating, living on borrowed time, getting to continue what he never had.

Jo Ann Stanley

The fog rises from the depths of the canyon, the mist expanding to cover the mountain in cloud. I can hear the river beneath his blanket. Early rays of sunshine burn through the wet and warm my shoulders. I lean back on a rock and breathe deeply.

The curtain lifts slowly. The stage is bigger than life and set with ancient buildings of stone that sprawl across the mountain's saddle. The rocks crumble with weeds and wildflowers.

There are no characters. The city exists only physically; there are no people to give life to the structure. It is a magnificent backdrop but a dead play.

I was twenty-one when I wrote these words in my journal. Twenty-one on the twenty first: my golden year. During that year of travel I truly came of age and discovered my essence, my core. I developed independence and self-confidence. That year I left home, family, college and security far behind and embraced adventure instead. I became a traveler; thought I was invincible. With a good friend and a green backpack, I went south to South America. The scene described in my journal was my first view of Machu Picchu in Peru. I had earned that privileged observation point above the stone city by hiking with gear for five days along the ancient Inca Highway, through rain and mud, at exhausting altitudes. As I rested at the Inca Gate, the scene below me was revealed, and I tried to write it down.

I was blessed with a happy childhood and loving parents. My name "Jo Ann" combines their two names; my dad was Joseph, my mom, Ruth Ann. Now that I am a parent myself, I can more fully appreciate the many ways they supported my siblings and me. They weren't perfect; my dad had a terrible temper, and my mom may have suffered from depression because she was often unhappy or tearful. Occasionally they were angry enough to spank us. Once or twice Dad was so mad at my brother that I remember him using his belt. But most of the time they were good to us, and they had the wisdom to support their children in their own choices, even though none of the four followed a very traditional path.

I grew up in Maryland, just outside Washington, D.C. My dad worked for Litton Industries, where he developed and marketed the altimeter. He was an electrical engineer with a degree in chemistry who built the first color TV in the neighborhood, from a Heathkit. Constantly tinkering with gadgets and technology, he installed a homemade intercom in our house. Every other Friday, when my parents played bridge across the street, Dad unrolled a huge wheel of wire to keep tabs on the frolicsome four over that intercom. In this way my thrifty parents avoided the expense of a babysitter.

My mom worked at home. She volunteered at the nursery school, drove the carpool, shopped, cooked the meals, and cleaned. She drew the line at ironing; we needed a hired woman named Millie for that. Like all of her siblings, she was good with words and had worked for the Department of Agriculture before she was married. Twenty years later after raising her four children, she went back to work-for the same boss. In all that time he never found anyone better.

When I was two, I fell from a brick retaining wall to the concrete floor at the outside door of our basement and fractured my skull. I lay in my parents' bed with a concussion. The doctors still made house calls then, so I never went to the hospital. Apparently I was lucky not to have brain damage. (Or maybe there was some?) At five, I was running in socks when I slipped on the kitchen floor and chipped my front tooth, my first permanent tooth. It was not cosmetically repaired until I was an adult. At the time I had a million freckles, a pixie haircut and a ridiculous home permanent given to me by my aunt. She also gave me hula lessons.

After I learned to read, I ceased to communicate with the outside world. Twice I was so involved in my book that I absent-mindedly pulled a lamp over onto my already soft head. My older brother Ray set a fire in the backyard, and John, the younger one, got caught lighting matches in the basement of a house under construction. Both had serious meetings with the local fire chief. My little sister Mary had to get glasses for a lazy eye when she was five years old. For some reason they were pink glasses with glitter. She also had a favorite cowgirl outfit that she wore almost every day. Of the four of us, John was the most accident-prone. He was running with a stick and punctured his palate; he was hit by a car while riding his bike and received a broken arm. Another time he got into a vicious poison ivy battle. John thought he was immune but soon found out that he wasn't. Weeks of horrific itching and festering pustules followed. I had a tonsillectomy and Ray had an appendectomy. I had impetigo, twice, from playing in the creek, a lovely little stream that must have been polluted. I didn't mind too much, because I got to stay home from school even though I didn't feel sick. Our mom was always telling us not to play in the creek, but I loved the meadow and the creek. One time a man exposed himself to my friend and me when we were playing there. That scared us enough to keep us away for a week. Of course we never told anyone.

On to adolescence. I got good grades, so my parents never bothered me about schoolwork. Reading was the first form of travel for me, and it remains my favorite pastime. In junior high, I played flute. One day our band leader actually stabbed himself in the arm with his baton. His face went white, and he had to leave the room. When I was thirteen I wrote in my diary that I wanted to kill myself, but instead I burned the diary. I hated my braces. I hated my freckles. My brother Ray, a childhood genius, built a sound-snooper of long metal tubes arranged in a spiral. He used this device to eavesdrop on one of my pajama parties, and afterwards, he blackmailed my girlfriends. So naturally, I hated my brother.

The summer after my ninth grade year, my brave parents took the entire family on a three-week road trip across this great country. We visited relatives in practically every state and all famous sites in between. We went to Chicago, the Black Hills, the Corn Palace. We floated in Salt Lake. We followed signs for miles until we got to Wall Drug Store. We visited the Badlands, Yellowstone, the Grand Tetons, Yosemite, the Pacific Ocean, Disneyland, and the Grand Canyon. For me and for Mary, John, and Ray, this trip remains the defining escapade in our family's life. There are a thousand stories from that jaunt, but only one major disaster:

We were crossing the desert in 100-degree weather when the car overheated. Dad pulled over and we all got out. When he lifted the hood, flames leapt from the engine. We panicked. Ray took off running for help. We had just passed a gas station about a mile back. (There were no cell phones in those days.) Mom yelled for us to get everything out of the car in case it burned up; then as soon as we got in and started grabbing suitcases she had a vision of the car exploding and screamed for us to get out. Someone driving by called out "Throw sand!" and suddenly we were dumping the desert on the engine. Meanwhile my brother had arrived in "town"—Tuba City, Arizona—and discovered some old men in rockers at the gas station. As he blurted out our predicament, panting, they proceeded to discuss it in frustrating detail, comparing it with every other incident of the past twenty years. Ray grabbed a fire extinguisher and started hoofing it back toward our car. I think the fire was out by the time Ray got there, but the car was definitely ruined. We then had the pleasure of spending the night in the Tuba City Motel, a dive like no other north of the border. My mom had a terror of creepy-crawlies and bed bugs that kept her up all that night. The next day we were towed over 75 miles to Flagstaff where we bought another car. My dad, having already blown his budget on the vacation itself, was reduced to making the best deal he could on a massive pink Buick. We breezed home in that bomb.

Actually my parents were making a smart purchase, because all through high school I was too embarrassed by our family vehicle to ever request the keys for that car. "Give me the Ghia, Dad." For several years we had the Buick, two Volkswagon Carmen Ghias, and an extra Ghia engine. My dad rotated the engines periodically to keep at least one of the Volkswagons running. If I was embarrassed by the pink car, my mother was mortified by the peeling paint on one of the Ghias. But the other one, the yellow one, that was the first car I ever loved.

In high school I met my future husband, Kerry Stanley. I was in tenth grade biology class when this bleached-blond surfer dude arrived tardy and took the seat next to me. He was starting school four days after Labor Day because he had been riding the waves in Cape Hatteras with friends. He was way too cool, and I immediately had a crush that never went away.

We were alphabetically destined. My maiden name is Spalding, so Stanley and I sat next to each other in approximately four classes a semester all through high school. We became very good friends. To get him to stop cracking his knuckles during trigonometry tests, I bribed him with Mounds bars. I never would have made it through physics without his notes. But generally, we traveled in different circles. He starred in school plays, had an older girlfriend who had won a major beauty contest, and was generally in with a more popular crowd. I was self-conscious, not exactly shy but not an attention-getter, still had braces, and a different group of friends. I began sharing a locker with my first boyfriend, Bruce, and fell in love with him. He was a poet, a free spirit, who charmed me with his theories. Because Bruce was a good friend of Kerry's we would sometimes double date with Kerry and his various girlfriends.

Around us the sixties were raging. Living in Washington, D.C. during the sixties was inevitably political. Every weekend we went down to the mall to stop the war and save the world. I heard Martin Luther King speak. I was almost arrested at the Justice Department. My parents had to pick me up at a police station when I was caught driving without a license. It didn't help that the reason I didn't have my license with me was because they had confiscated it when they grounded me. There was a lot of tension between my parents and me during those years. The sixties framed the inevitable teen years of risk and rebellion for me.

As it happened, Kerry and I were the only two students from our high school to go away to Antioch College in Ohio. We continued as close friends, spending time with each other at school, making new friends there and traveling back and forth together to Washington for visits with family and our respective love interests.

It was a great year. I enjoyed my college classes and loved hiking in Glen Helen, the 1,000 acres of virgin forest adjacent to the campus. At night friends would walk into town for hot whole-wheat donuts. Antioch had an intern program and for one quarter I worked with mentally retarded adults at Camphill Village in New York State. This work, as well as earlier volunteer work at a community center in D.C., is part of what led me into teaching. At Antioch I also became very close to my roommate, Kim, from Massachusetts. But somehow by the end of the year we all wanted to leave school and get on with life.

While I was at Antioch, my dad lost his job at Litton. His entire department was laid off; even though he was the head of the department, he went too. Although he eventually found other work, my dad never really recovered from this blow to his ego and career. I started feeling guilty about spending so much of his money to be at an expensive college, or maybe that was a convenient excuse, because my parents never wanted me to leave school. But I thought it was a waste of their money because I didn't know what I wanted to study, and what I really wanted to do was to see more of the world. At the end of the year, I left Antioch. So did Kerry, for his own reasons.

My desire to see more of the world sparked a new pattern. A slave to my wanderlust, I worked at various jobs, saved all my money, then took a trip. I spent a semester in Mexico at *La Universidad de Las Americas*, and fell in love with Latin America and the Spanish language. I saved up my money and took that backpacking trip to South America. I was gone for eight months. Then I saved for another year and went to Europe. After traveling all over Europe, wintering in Greece, and visiting my aunt Helen in Istanbul, Turkey, where she lived, I finally decided I wanted to finish college.

You won't be surprised that my parents agreed to pay tuition only at the University of Maryland, about five minutes away from the family home. I enrolled and began to study literature. Later, when I thought about what I might do with my degree, I wandered into teaching. I graduated with a degree in English Education and a minor in Spanish. I had a fabulous student teaching experience in the best high school English department ever and in May I was hired for the following year. I taught both English and Spanish there for the next nine years, loving my job and learning so much from my colleagues, to whom I am still indebted. At night I earned my master's degree in English. Teaching remains my vocation.

All this time Kerry and I had been orbiting around each other. We had both been involved in other relationships, but we managed never to lose touch with each other. When the timing was right, our connection became stronger. I truly believe that the beauty of our marriage today and for the past seventeen years has much to do with how close we were as friends from the day we met.

We were married in 1986 at the Strong Mansion on Sugar Loaf Mountain outside Washington, D.C. About 100 friends and relatives were witnesses to this momentous occasion. Our friends created a beautiful wedding for us. The invitations, the photography, the cake, the music, the ceremony itself, were all gifts from friends and from my mom. I'm sorry my dad had already passed away and couldn't be there in person, but he had to be watching. My brother Ray walked me down the aisle. My brother John escorted my mother, and my sister Mary was my maid of honor.

About a year after we were married, Kerry and I moved to New Jersey to be near his office. I interviewed and got a teaching job at a high school in Haddonfield, NJ. When I started my new job in the fall, there was one thing I didn't tell my employers right away. I was pregnant! Kerry and I were ready for rug rats.

My two babies were born in south Jersey, where there are still enough farms to retain the claim "Garden State." We lived in a unique town in the Pinelands called Medford Lakes, a community of log cabins, woods, and cedar lakes. It's the only place I know of that celebrates a Canoe Carnival each year. There is a festival of lights on one of the lakes on Friday night, when everyone in the community is out on the lake in his or her own boat. On Saturday night friends and neighbors gather on the beaches to watch a parade of elaborate floats on canoes. My children and I spent their toddler years reading stories on the couch in our PJs, wading in the lakes, and walking in the woods. I still miss our friends from those years.

I lost both my parents too young. My dad had a massive heart attack when he was 70, and my mom died of cancer when she was 65. My kids never knew my parents. My mom babysat only once for my eldest daughter, when Corinne was only a few months old. Kerry has also lost his parents. His mom died of lung disease the day we were scheduled to move into our new house in New Jersey, so although she knew we were expecting a baby,she never met her granddaughters. Kerry and his brothers were with her in the hospital, but I was alone in a cold empty house waiting for the movers when Kerry called to tell me that she had passed. His dad, the only one of our parents who got to know his grandchildren, died of emphysema when my younger daughter, Brooke, was in kindergarten. This is the downside of being late bloomer Baby Boomers.

We moved to the Kansas City metro for Kerry to pursue a promotion while the kids were still in elementary school. We learned that the steaks and barbecue live up to reputation, that contrary to popular belief, there are some hills in Kansas, that Midwestern values are good for children, and that Dorothy was really saying something when she said "There's no place like home." We discovered the Westwood View community and the advantages of a superb school district, Shawnee Mission. I have been able to spend time with my children as they have grown while maintaining my career interests through a series of interesting part-time writing and teaching options. I've also recently re-fired my passion for the Spanish language, and am using Spanish both at home and in my work.

I have a good life, wonderful friends, a long haired cat, and a Golden Retriever. Kerry has a fabulous job, which he enjoys, and he still plays his guitar every night. Kerry and I have two beautiful and gifted daughters: Corinne, who is already sixteen and in high school, and Brooke, who is a spirited fourteen. I love them deeply.

That's my life story in a nutshell. But that's not the only story. I have other stories to tell. As I look to the future, I plan to write more and sleep less.

LOOKING AHEAD

What's Next

There are beginnings and there are endings.
What meaning and effect your experience here will have in your life—
only you will ultimately know.
The responsibility as always, is yours to make of it what you will.
Bon voyage, my friends.

—John Hurst

Patricia Antonopoulos

You know that light at the end of all those tunnels? That light we are supposed to see as we negotiate the darker airless parts of life? Well, I think I must have kept my eyes closed a lot. And now I absolutely do not want to see the light at the end. I like the now.

What I have learned along the way are those bits of knowledge that are supposed to move me into a better future. But I am not going. I plan to stay right here.

There are whole chapters of my life that might have been different had I understood that the now was far more important than anything I could project into the future.

Children need love far more than they need admonishment. . . and we are all children of someone. Whatever harm is done to a child is not a moment in time—it is a lifetime moment.

Living each belief can earn disciples, while mismatching the talk and the walk invites alienation.

For many women, the relationship with food can be a barometer of emotional health. And this relationship with food is profaned by the belief that our form matches our function. We need to accept our bodies as our containers and not our value packs.

Often the need to be right is based on the fear that someone will discover our inadequacies. Anger owns our spirit and that spirit can be painted with the brush strokes of our anger weapons.

Many women need a sense of intimacy before sex and men often experience that sense of intimacy after sex. Who missed that design flaw?

My spiritual journey has taken me to some of those roads less traveled. Often I searched in anguish, begging any listening Higher Power for direction. There were times I searched with what smelled like intellectual arrogance, wanting just the provable facts.

And I am not there yet—not anywhere, really. But I believe that the destination is here, not there.

And I plan to continue.

Patti Dickinson

I am completely geographically challenged. I have lived in Kansas City for more than half my life, and I have yet to leave the house for a trip to the airport without a few pangs of "What if I can't remember which highway, and I wind up in San Diego?" I know right and left; I don't know I-70, 435 or 35.

Therefore, I'm thinking that a geographical approach to this topic is a bit risky for someone like me. But, for the most part, I think my "What nexts" are all about the roads I didn't take, the exits I didn't get off on. You might say, I'm just circling around again.

The road not taken #1: the Peace Corps. Instead, I think that I might try a mission trip with a couple of my high school kids. I'm pretty good with the gritty parts of life. I'm even better at rolling up my shirtsleeves and making things happen.

The road not taken #2: a front porch. I am going to learn how to sit and watch the world go by. Live in the moment. Slow down. Knit, read. Think. Write. Grandchildren. Finding a niche.

Shawna Samuel

I've always been a planner, a dreamer. I like living a life I feel like I'm building upon. And I always think the best is just around the corner. When the phone rings, I'm sure it's something fun to do. When I think of the future, I'm sure it's going to be great. I dream of my kids turning out to be the wonderful people I know they are inside. I imagine them as successful, happy and healthy adults. Mostly I imagine that we'll like each other, and that grandchildren will bring me some of my happiest days. I really look forward to being a grandma. I think Duncan and I will be stupendous grandparents. The kind that are at every ball game and dance recital. The kind that make cookies before dinner, allow jumping on the bed, and enjoy hour-long walks just up the street and back. The kind who are never too hurried to read a book aloud, or listen to a problem.

I think a career is in my future. I imagine a creative, challenging and fun job that I feel passionate about. And I imagine working with wonderful new people, my future friends. I imagine Duncan blossoming without the stress and demands of his career. I see him filling up his buckets that have been empty for so long, filling them up with his own alone time, creative fulfillment, and just having enough time to think and feel grounded. I look forward to the husband and father he will be when his buckets are full and he's leading a more balanced life.

I look forward to the contentment of older age, of feeling satisfaction that I've done that, the chapter is complete, and feeling peaceful about it. I'm looking forward to the drive diminishing, when that day comes. I'm looking forward to feeling less involved with the material, and more involved with inner peace. I'm looking forward to enjoying friendships that have spanned decades, being there to listen and support, to see all of us go through the different passages of life.

I want to be fit and active as an old lady, with short silver hair, a bit of a tan from being outside so much and brightly painted fingernails. I want to learn more about gardening, house projects and maybe travel more. I want to have character, a lot of wrinkles from laughing a lot (no frown wrinkles or Botox for me). I want to have a sparkle in my eyes and be fun to be around. I want to feel comfortable in my own skin and with who I've become, but without feeling like I've ever totally arrived so I'll continue to grow, change and be interesting. I want a simple life filled with love and the pleasures of living.

I guess I want a lot. You won't find a Mercedes or a bigger house on my list of dreams, but I have a tall order in the "what counts" department. I suppose my view of the future is a true definition of a through and through optimist because I truly, truly believe that these things will happen. I admit, there is a small little shadow of doubt in my head that can occasionally flash a picture of doom, like the other shoe is just waiting to drop; things are just too good to be true. But I do not invite it in. I continue to believe with all my heart that good things are around the corner and will come in their due time.

Even with my strong hopes for a good future, I don't live in the future. I still have both feet firmly planted in the here and now. Because the way I see it, the only way to get to my dreams of the future is to live each day I'm given now to the absolute fullest, and just keep on plugging.

Jo Ann Stanley

What's next? Increasingly, I find myself contemplating retirement. Never mind that I haven't accomplished any of my lifelong goals, like writing a book or seeing my kids through college. My husband and I haven't even seen our children through adolescence, yet I find myself catapulting over the next twelve or fifteen years and dreaming about the two of us living the life of leisure.

There's a property on the water in North Carolina, not on the ocean, but near, on the Albemarle Sound. The house we'll buy is weathered gray from the salty air. Our windows look out over the blue water on one side and toward the town marina on the other, with its modest collection of sailboats. The marina might be busy on Saturdays with boat owners, kids, and crabbers baiting their lines with chicken necks. But mostly it's quiet there in our home between the Sound and the woods where we read our books. On the private side of the house the green lawn slopes gracefully down to the water's edge, where a weeping willow trails in the water and impatiens grow in the shade.

Mornings we rise early, breakfast quickly and ride our bikes through the wooded lanes or take long walks ocean-side. On the beach, our feet sink in the sand and we enjoy the waves pounding, gulls screeching, pelicans diving; often, we'll see the dolphins. Then on our lawn we'll sit in white Adirondack chairs, sipping coffee as we watch the ospreys dive for fish or circle their nests, nests they have built high up on small platforms on poles in the bay. Days are for errands and projects, but in the evening when the sun sets over the Sound we'll visit together as we sip our wine and nibble bruschetta. When night falls and the stars emerge, he'll play his guitar and sing the old songs. Then we'll get ready for bed and fall asleep in each other's arms, just as we always have.

Each summer and sometimes at Christmas, the girls will come with their families to visit because if we live at the beach they'll always come to see us and we rarely have to travel to visit them, unless there's a new grandbaby.

In Spain the word for retirement is "jubliacíon," a cognate for "jubilation." Like the Spanish, I envision my retirement as a period of joy and contentment. There's no stress, no arguments, no teenage angst, no devastating health issues, no financial concerns, and no war to mar my romance. My husband is always by my side, and my children lead fulfilled lives. When I'm ready, death comes to me in my sleep, and I sail away on a cloud.

REFLECTION

A Closing Thought

Yet I could never explain how the image and the reality merge,
and how they somehow extend and beautify each other.

—**Dodie Smith,** *I Capture the Castle*

Patricia Antonopoulos

*I*t is time to merge our group reality with our longstanding dream. Have we enriched one another? Magnified what is best in each of us?

We came together as friends of circumstance, the way of most beginnings, the hope for a lifetime circle of friendship. There were struggles as we learned to value the promised privacy, to trust in that privacy. We shared fragments of stories as we worked our way towards the strength of more complete sharing.

Our personalities have surface similarities, but there were also deep differences honed by hurts and successes along our individual paths. We dabbled in judgment of self and others, as we struggled with the realization that we loved all of life and so could not love nor expect perfection.

As we tried to merge judgment with acceptance, we felt the tightness. And so there were subjects we left alone, avoiding both writings and discussions.

And as the months grew to years, the circle did feel safe, the friendships true and lasting. These were the months to years that were truly focused in on strength, courage and writing. Friendship was steady, as sturdy as the cycle of the sun.

A single piece of writing took us into those deep differences and wrenched some new reality. We could be cracked by our inability to agree on a profound level. On this piece of writing, we divided, unable to look dispassionately at the consequences. A stranger was asked to heal the breach.

The drift had begun and separation felt inevitable. Changes were subtle but intense. We handled it sadly as we moved towards a new reality.

No more twice each month protected dates on the calendar. No more time to share our lives as a treasured priority. Now we were a book group, a come-if-you-can group.

There were changes in work lives, careers demanding more time, more attention, more focus. There is little time for anything but friendship of circumstance. Now we are about the book.

For some of us, there was intense belief in our book. Heart and spirit were invested right along with the years. We had held to one another through births, illness, crises, death and all that comes within. Together, we cried, laughed, shared and cared for one another to the depths that we knew.

But the drift had begun and the dissolution seemed inevitable. The group was gone, but the memories will be with me until my death.

One friendship will be an exception. Patti has been my source of comfort beyond measure. We have walked a common ground, cementing my belief that it is possible to find that person who can listen, accept, encourage, guide and gently redirect when needed. Our friendship will not be a memory.

Years.

Wonderful, incredible, amazing years.

Years which did hold more promise, more reality than I expected in the beginning.

Years spent with women of courage and conviction as well as remarkable talents.

We have learned, grown, changed. The image and the reality of our group did merge into a thing of beauty that has influenced our lives—a glorious friendship of circumstance.